"Amanda Lea Kaiser has given us the quintessential playbook for engagement—from the member's perspective. When you're reading, it's as if you're really listening to members talk about their journeys and their expectations from those journeys. From the time your members join and observe your association, to the time they lead and advocate on its behalf, this playbook is invaluable to your engagement development strategy. Bravo, Amanda! This goes in the 'stoooopid-good' category!"

REGGIE HENRY, CAE, chief information and performance excellence officer, ASAE: The Center for Association Leadership

"*Elevating Engagement* provides a step-by-step guide to creating and enhancing member connection. From the simplest ideas to the most complex strategies, Amanda Lea Kaiser has written a definitive guide for all association leaders."

MARY BYERS, author, *Race for Relevance: 5 Radical Changes for Associations*

"Amanda Lea Kaiser has taken the mystery out of driving member engagement using community-centered thinking. Kaiser expertly outlines what to do to ensure great member experiences and what it takes to empower members to do more than just pay their dues. This is a must-read for association leaders and membership professionals."

MARJORIE ANDERSON, founder, Community by Association

"Experiences have always been important, but today they are essential. In *Elevating Engagement*, Amanda Lea Kaiser guides us through the six stages of member engagement using her expert observations, tried-and-true tips, and relatable examples. If you work or volunteer for an association, I highly recommend adding this book to your must-read list."

SHERI JACOBS, CEO and president,
Avenue M Group

"Amanda Lea Kaiser is a keen observer of what true member engagement looks like and the subtle forces that drive it. This book is chock-full of practical advice on how to capture your members' attention and keep them coming back for more. It belongs on every association leader's shelf!"

MADDIE GRANT, digital strategist; author,
The Non-Obvious Guide to Employee Engagement

"I finished *Elevating Engagement* and immediately started reading it again, this time scribbling madly in a notebook to capture all the ideas that it sparked in me. I can tell that Amanda Lea Kaiser's thought leadership is going to have a major influence on what it means to run inclusive and welcoming associations that foster true belonging. I hope so—because the world will be a better place for it."

ARIANNA REHAK, CEO and co-founder,
Matchbox Virtual Media

6/27/24

L: 2.

You Go, LEO!!!

~Amanda

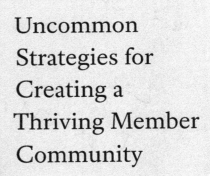

Uncommon Strategies for Creating a Thriving Member Community

Amanda Lea Kaiser

elevating
engagement

Cataloguing in publication information is available from Library and Archives Canada.
ISBN 978-1-77458-326-5 (paperback)
ISBN 978-1-77458-327-2 (ebook)

Page Two
pagetwo.com

Edited by Erin Parker
Copyedited by Crissy Calhoun
Proofread by Melissa Kawaguchi
Cover and interior design by Fiona Lee
Interior illustrations by Amanda Lea Kaiser

AmandaLeaKaiser.com

For Jeff and Gavin,
who are my co-conspirators
in the very best adventures.

contents

introduction

"The world of the future is in our making. Tomorrow is now."

ELEANOR ROOSEVELT

HAD JUST spent four hours battling traffic, with the sun in my eyeballs, to attend what I called Solopreneur Camp in upstate New York. By the time I pulled into the parking lot, I was kind of frazzled and had a splitting headache. I took a minute to clean off the passenger seat, collect my stuff, stow the granola bar wrappers, and steel myself for an event that was now starting to feel waaaaayyyyy out of my comfort zone. I expected to have a few more minutes of quiet time to get myself and my stuff together before entering the fray. I was wrong.

I opened my door and a woman in a sunny orange T-shirt popped out from behind my car, accosting me with a huge smile, and happily shouted, "HI THERE!!!" I almost fainted. Well, I didn't *really* almost faint, but had I been a cartoon character, that's exactly what would have happened.

Before I could jump back in my car and speed away, the lady chirped, "How long was your trip?" while grabbing my wheelie bag out of the trunk. Another car drove by and a wave of dust from the parking lot rolled over us, but she seemed unfazed. "Follow me! I'll show you the way." We chatted all the way across the parking lot.

I was so engrossed in the conversation that I was surprised when a giant bubble floated between us. At the camp entrance, volunteers demonstrated the art of making two-handed *giant* bubbles. You know the kind: they stretch five feet until they snap-seal and form this enormous, transparent, wobbly blob. My greeter said, "You've got to try this," while someone else handed me a wand.

I mimicked their technique and lucked out when my bubble spanned the path, peeled away from the wand, and lazily floated off over the parking lot. This elicited whoops and hollers from the band of merry volunteers. "I think you get the prize for the biggest bubble so far," one told me.

Just then a bus pulled in, and a swarm of volunteers ran to it cheering and gleefully welcoming the road-worn travelers. The woman with my stuff beamed at me again and said, "Come on, let's get you settled." Our conversation picked right back up where we'd left off as we headed into the camp.

Outside the registration area, my new friend said, "I'll watch your stuff. Head on in there and they will get you a schedule and a few other things." Inside a barn-like building, I took my place in line behind the other new arrivals. Volunteers were welcoming us with enthusiasm, walking us through the program, and handing out swag bags. When I popped back outside, the greeter escorted me to my cabin, pointing out activities of interest along the way. "Once you get settled, feel free to come back out here and join a game or do some crafts. I like the temporary tattoo table the best! See my dragon?" It was a very beautiful, sparkly teal dragon; I suddenly wanted one too. My headache now magically gone, I could take in my surroundings. As I scanned the quad, everyone—volunteers and campers alike—seemed genuinely happy, as well as a little quirky and fun. *Hmmm*, I thought, *perhaps I've found my peeps?*

This conference was very much like other conferences in that there were keynote speeches, too many servings of rubbery chicken (even one is too many), arctic-cold break-out session rooms, lanyards of an awkward length, and networking. What was noticeably different was the experience. For five days, there was magic in the air and a sense of limitless energy, excitement, and possibility, all supported by the activities the hosts planned. The event host told me that with every decision they made, they kept imagining how attendees would feel. How would attendees feel after traveling all day? How would attendees feel when they stepped onto the property not knowing anyone else? How would attendees feel after a long day of learning, connecting, and sharing?

Hundreds of small decisions culminated in an experience that generated a super positive attendee culture, making everyone feel like they'd just met 373 new BFFs. After its inaugural year, this conference attracted people from Australia, Japan, and other far-flung locales and spurred one of the most active online communities I've seen. The vetted speakers, fun swag, and property made the conference good. But the curated experiences made it great.

Connoisseur of Experiences, at Your Service

Everyone notices their experiences, but I am a connoisseur of experiences. Parented by a customer-service-whiz mom and a dad whose engineering brain tuned in to details most people walked right by, I was unintentionally groomed to notice human interactions from an early age. In everyday life, I make it my mission to notice experiences—mine, friends', family members', and even strangers'. I pay attention to what it feels like walking through the door of the cute little boutique store. I dissect the impact of well-designed home pages. From appliance deliveries to chitchats with the mail carriers at my local post office, I examine each experience to figure out what organizations and leaders are doing right and how they can improve.

This is not only a personal fascination but a professional one. Early in my marketing career, I had the opportunity to guide the Crayola brand, and every day I saw firsthand how experiences with the iconic and beloved art materials shaped consumers' feelings and drove loyalty. In a different role, as the director of marketing and membership at a professional association, I had the opportunity to conduct interviews with members and learn what made them tick. Nowadays, as an independent researcher, keynote speaker, and consultant, I talk to members about their experiences all the time. While giving interactive presentations with chapter or affiliate leaders, running problem-solving events, facilitating collaborative innovation labs, or conducting member interviews (477 and counting, for thirty-three separate research studies!), I've learned a lot about what professionals want in their careers, for their organizations, and from their associations—and I've closely studied the impact of members' experiences on decision-making.

I suspect that members feel that talking to me is a lot like having an intimate conversation with a stranger on an airplane. They can reveal their deepest feelings because they don't know me and they will never cross paths with me again. I'm the anonymous and friendly seatmate who inspires members to share stories they've never shared with anyone else about their careers, lives, and member journeys. These stories have taught me two important lessons:

1 How emotional both the world of work and the member journey can be. Because we rely on data and metrics and stats, it can be hard to remember that there is a person, behavior, and a pile of beautiful and messy feelings behind every one of those numbers.

2 What a powerful impact experiences have on engagement with member associations, now more than ever before.

The Rising Importance of Member Experiences

Experiences drive emotions, and emotions drive members' decisions to engage. (Boom! Mic drop!) So, what does this mean? Creating exceptional experiences is the key to capturing our members' hearts and then minds. This is especially true today, as the world of work is changing very rapidly, putting more and more pressure on members—extreme pressure. If we want to be a part of our members' lives, we must understand this new reality and adapt to it.

Once upon a time, maintaining membership was a breeze. When typewriters clacked, memos were distributed by inter-office mail, and lunchtime was for socializing—that was perhaps the golden age of associations. Employers paid for dues, conferences, meetings, and travel as well as allocating time for service and volunteer activities. In many industries and professions, there was an implicit rule that joining was expected.

Back then, members abided by behaviors that sustained their associations. Members tended to join and stay members for years. Once they'd gotten the hang of things at the association, they often sought out leadership opportunities.

Sometimes there were more volunteers than spots available. Members quickly learned to turn to the association first when they needed the latest information or had a question.

But things have changed—a lot! Members, like the associations they belong to, are different now. Corporate hierarchies are condensing, leaving middle managers with more responsibility. Industries are continually trying to carve out more efficiency, straining their processes and workers. Magnifying glasses are searching for every seemingly extraneous expense, so projects are perpetually underfunded. The race to be first means shorter, often unreasonable deadlines. Nearly every professional feels the conflicting pressures of having less time to produce more with fewer resources. The typical pressures of today's work world force us into a reactionary stance; there is no time for strategic thinking. There are never enough minutes to plan, analyze, eat (or pee) between meetings, or look much further into the future than the mountain of work coming straight at us.

When strategic brain time is at a premium, people rely on their intuition and underlying feelings to determine where to find information they can trust, which mission to get behind, and where to belong. It takes too long to compare features and benefits and calculate value. Instead, people apply heuristics or their internal rules of thumb as shortcuts to decide if they should join, attend, purchase, or renew.

Here are some of the shortcuts members employ:

- Will I be safe in this community?
- Do people like me join associations like this?
- What were my first impressions of this association?
- Will I enjoy belonging to this community?

Like most psychological heuristics, these mental short-cuts run in the subconscious. Members might be unaware of these mental models in play, so when we ask members why they joined, they are likely to retrospectively validate their decisions with logic. "I joined for the networking opportunities," they say. Or "I joined to attend the conference." Or "I joined for the education offerings." And while logic does play a role, the feelings that inform the decision play an outsized one. It is their experiences that create these emotions.

If we could see the actual inputs to the decision to engage in action, we might see thoughts like *They seem nice* or *This feels safe* or *She seems a lot like me.*

Unless negative emotions were triggered. In that case your member may have just disengaged.

We must anticipate these normal feelings before they happen and change the script, which means changing the focus of association leaders, staff, and volunteers.

Creating great experiences is the new art of engagement. Engagement is no longer just about boosting and communicating value. Engagement happens when members see the value to them *and* when they have great experiences. This book is about how to cultivate, curate, and create experiences for members because the experience side of engagement is one of the biggest opportunities for associations today.

A focus on your members' experiences can start right now. You can do experience work before or in tandem with mission, value, or technology projects. You won't need a big budget (or any budget for that matter). And you don't even need a series of board approvals to make your members' experiences a priority.

Focusing on your members' experience is not an all-or-nothing game. We're not talking about a huge seismic shift in culture tomorrow. No massive strategic document is needed. Instead, member experience experiments can be as small or as big as you wish, depending on your capacity. As slow or fast too. One person can effectively use these strategies, or you can roll them out to teams or the whole association.

Whether you get there quickly or slowly, one at a time or all together, we are seeing a new trend. The boards and staff of future associations will assume a new role where member experience takes center stage.

The new role I invite you to try on is Chief Experience Officer.

As the Chief Experience Officer (CEO) of your association, you will put on your members' shoes and slip on their glasses to walk the world seeing things through their eyes. You will consider every experience, from the application process to attending a conference to reading emails and more. As this kind of CEO, you might find a new optimism in the freedom to create, the excitement of adventure, and the hopefulness of new opportunities. (I realize the acronym is a little confusing! You can totally be an association CEO and also take on this new role of CEO, but you don't have to be *the* CEO to also become a CEO. Follow me?)

Are you concerned that you're not ready for this new role? I've totally got your back! In fact, this book is packed with one bazillion (approximately one bazillion two hundred and thirty-three, give or take a dozen or so) tips for every step of the way. Consider me your exuberant, happy-go-lucky tour guide of our members' journey.

The Six Stages of Member Engagement

Over the years, I've talked to new members and longtime members, members at various places in their careers and on different rungs of the corporate ladder. I have interviewed university presidents, rocket scientists (also rock scientists), and all different types of engineers, as well as people working for publishing corporations, finance companies, and government bureaus like NASA, just to name a few. No matter the profession, industry, or field, members tend to want and need similar things as they progress through their member journey, and that journey usually involves six distinct stages of engagement.

In this book, we are going to explore each stage from our members' point of view as a way to reverse-engineer engagement and create a richer member experience. Pulling from my research and member conversations, we will uncover the go and no-go decisions that members often make at each stage.

Here are the six stages in a trapezoid-shaped nutshell:

Observe

Assess

Participate

Contribute

Collaborate

Lead

Observe: Starting at the moment they click Join, new members actively observe everything they can about the association. They're wondering, *Did I make a mistake?* Observing members are watching, reading, and hoping.

Assess: Members start to layer judgment on top of their observations. Each new member is trying to determine if the association is for people like them.

Participate: Members dip their toes into the water and share little bits of their knowledge and thoughts in small ways. They participate in a virtual event chat. They raise their hand during a session. They may even respond to a question in the online community. As they do this, they're learning if participating is safe.

Contribute: Members graduate from quick chats and posts to more substantive contributions. They may write an article, speak at a conference, or sit for a video interview. It takes more time and energy to contribute, and contributors quickly learn if their contributions are valued.

Collaborate: This is the most overlooked member engagement stage. Every industry or profession has problems that are not easily solved with education or research, but some members realize that perhaps by working as a team, more great minds can do together what one member cannot do alone.

Lead: In what is often thought of as the volunteer stage, leaders occupy roles like board member, committee member, organizer, and advocate.

I've listed the six stages of engagement in the most common sequence. However, you might find some of your members take a different path. Members nearly always start off in the Observe and Assess stages, and then they might skip or reverse steps, and that's okay. A new member might love the community so much they start contributing or leading right away. Or you might find that because they've cut steps, they're not as engaged in their current stage as they might have been had they progressed through the stages in order.

The stages are not time dependent. Some members may observe for three days while others stay in this stage for six years. While we can give members every opportunity to level up, they don't want to be forcefully rushed or held back.

Each chapter of this book is dedicated to a different stage of engagement, and it's brought to life with a story from our fictional hero, Kat Taylor. Kat's stories are a composite of hundreds of stories that members have shared with me over the years, with details and names changed for confidentiality. Other member anecdotes and stories from my own experiences are sprinkled throughout the book to show you what these ideas and challenges might look like in action.

If you are an association leader interested in engagement, this book is for you. By *leader*, I mean association staff, board members, and chapter leaders. You might lead a professional or trade association. Your association may be large, medium, or small, with regional or international reach, or a society, professional community, or chapter. Most of the insights are universal to all types and sizes of associations, but there are some nuances; when it makes sense, I flag specific strategies for a particular kind of association (e.g., "Hey, trade association leaders, you might like this idea!"). In the following pages, we'll cover all types of engagement including new-member engagement, engaging marketing, attendee engagement, online community engagement, and volunteer engagement.

You are welcome to read this book sequentially for a plunge into all things member engagement. Walking through the stages in order will show you how engagement builds as members progress on their journey. But reading this book from cover to cover is not the only way to enjoy it. I also invite you to skip around if you want to focus on a specific stage of membership. If you think it's time to update your new-member onboarding program, skim the Observe and Assess chapters. If you are exploring ways to gain more engagement in your online communities and at your events, start with Participate. Looking for new voices to speak, write, and be interviewed? Try Contribute. Are you ready for a new kind of interaction with your members? I heartily recommend Collaborate. When you want ideas about increasing volunteer engagement, head over to Lead.

WE HAVE so many more opportunities to engage members than we think we have. It is so easy to get hemmed in by what we've always done, the structure we've created, the skills we use, and the commonly held definition of what an association is. Sometimes it is difficult to see a different path. My job is to shine a light on 152 different paths (exactly 152), all of which have something in common.

As we think about where we want to take our associations and societies in the future, the key to all good things is member engagement. Engagement drives acquisition, retention, purchases, registrations, content contributions, and volunteerism. Great associations are great because of enthusiastic member engagement. Associations die from lack of engagement.

Every day I become a more passionate advocate for engagement because I believe that associations are perfectly positioned to make a huge difference in the world of work. Imagine your association becoming known as the soul of the industry or the benevolent mentor of the profession. Imagine how empowering it would be for professionals to feel that your association is the supportive teacher/therapist/coach/guru/cheerleader/friend who is there for them 24/7. That would be great, right? But first we need to get really, really good at genuine, authentic, big-hearted engagement.

1

observe

"A smile is a curve that
sets everything straight."

PHYLLIS DILLER

KAT FEELS like she's drowning. Since her promotion six months ago, her job has gone from a consistent hum of activity to a chaotic swarm of work flying at her from all angles. She's easily putting in twelve-hour days while not making a dent in her "real" work because of all the meetings. Oh gosh, the meetings! A never-ending stream of meetings from 6 a.m. until 6 p.m., with late nights and weekends thrown in for good measure.

When Kat is not in a meeting, she's talking on the phone with one of her thirty-seven direct reports or trying desperately to make some headway on one of her many projects. It seems like no matter how long and hard she works these days, she's falling behind.

Niggling away at the back of her mind is worry about all her unopened emails. There are always at least four hundred in her inbox; today that number is at almost two thousand. She knows that her inability to keep up with the surge of email is just exacerbating the meeting problem, but she can't seem to get ahead of it. Kat wants to be the type of manager who puts her team first, but she feels she is letting everyone down by being so nonresponsive to email.

One day over lunch with Shelley, the main contact at her favorite vendor, Kat talks about some of the challenges she is wrestling with. "Have you checked out the association?"

Shelley says. "I have learned a lot from the community, which saved me a lot of time. Other customers tell me that the association is the place to go for new ideas." Kat isn't sure how she's going to swing any extra time (even if it does save her time in the end), but if Shelley vouches for them, Kat decides she should investigate the association. In no time at all, Kat's admin takes care of setting her up with digital access to the association, and soon the emails start trickling in.

On a good day, Kat can allocate sixty minutes for processing email, and she rapidly deletes as many as she can. The emails that go into the "deserves a read and maybe a response" pile are emails from her boss, other colleagues at her level, and three direct reports who work on big projects with full-company visibility. Normally, Kat would ignore all other emails, but there's something different about the emails coming from the association. It's like these folks are reading her mind. Not snooping around her brain in a creepy way, but in the supportive way your best friend says, "I totally hear you!" with their whole being.

The emails from the association are short, entertaining, and affirming. Someone is speaking her language, which is rare. Each message is worth a lot more than the thirty seconds she puts into reading it. Kat decides to temporarily add messages from the association to her "deserves a read" list, and she starts to look forward to these emails, which are a small beacon of calm in her otherwise frantic life.

· · · · ·

IMMEDIATELY BEFORE and after a member joins a new community, they like to get the lay of the land. In some sense, they want to know they are safe. Newcomers to a reception recede into the background so they can sip their drink and watch. Audience members observe the speaker before they volunteer to participate. Even during virtual events, first-time attendees often read the chat before typing their own thoughts.

Observing gives new members all kinds of cues.

They quickly get a sense of value. *Will this association help me?*

They get a sense of the level of professionalism. *Is this association as professional as I am?*

They get a sense of future belonging. *Could these folks be friends one day?*

But mostly, at this stage, prospective and new members wonder if joining will turn out to be the right decision. *Is this association worth my time and money? Do I feel cautiously optimistic, or do I feel like I'm going to regret this decision?* Our first split-second observations can lead us to hasty conclusions.

While members are making the decision to join, as they apply, and immediately after, they observe everything. Early on, all touchpoints between your association and members are important because each is a puzzle piece that starts to form an overall impression.

Sign Up Members without Them Checking Out

Let's put ourselves in the shoes of a prospective member as they browse the association website for the first time. What features might catch their eye? They'll take in the design of the website, the tone of the copy. They might read a brief article or watch a short video and scan the new-member leaderboard. They'll notice how everything looks, sounds, and feels. They might gaze at the images to find members like them or wonder if the pictures are stock photos. Prospective members will notice how well the website works on their phone or if it is hard to navigate.

They'll make observations about how easy it is to understand membership types or tiers and whether it seems like a simple or complicated and time-consuming process to sign up.

Eric couldn't believe how long the member application form was. Why were they asking him all these questions? Why were birth date and gender required fields? His institution had pulled questions like this from their registration forms long ago. He slogged his way through the form, dug out his company credit card, and hit Submit. He checked his watch. Signing up had taken over fifteen minutes, and he was almost late for a meeting. Run-walking to his meeting, Eric couldn't help but think, *Crikey! This association is a big black hole that I'm going to throw my time into.* If his boss, Joyce, hadn't recommended it and his company hadn't paid the fee, he would have quit twelve minutes ago.

Imagine you are a prospective member about to join your association. Is the process time-consuming, confusing, or unwelcoming? What can you change to make prospective members feel like joining is a snap, the association is up-to-date, and the community is friendly?

Escape the First Email Traps

Immediately after they join, new members eagerly observe everything about the association. This is when they're the most receptive to email messages. They scan or read these emails looking for clues, trying to get a sense of the association, and deciding whether or not they made a mistake by joining. They scroll from top to bottom, they click the links, they look at the fine print. Each email gets the royal treatment.

Each of the first three emails you send, that is.

That's right! Those first three emails are absolutely, monumentally, heart-stoppingly critical because they set up each new member for success or failure.

This is so important; I'll say it again: *Associations only have three emails to engage a new member!!!* Did your hair just stand on end? No worries, brush it back into place, because we can fix this!

When the first three emails are engaging, new members realize that messages from the association are valuable to them, and they'll keep reading them.

Unfortunately, when the first three emails are not engaging, new members mentally flip the switch in their brain that says it's okay to delete, file away, or wait for later to read these emails. Every time your association's name appears in their inbox, they know it's safe to ignore the message. Before you know it, seven months have passed, and because your new member hasn't read a single email, they haven't engaged with the association one tiny bit.

The usual association email cycle can be very damaging to engagement for new members. Only the most tenacious or supported members make it through.

Have you ever wondered why new members often join and then don't do *anything*? They don't log on; they don't read emails or articles or research; they never come to an event. Maybe it's because they are ignoring your email. Once new members start ignoring, it is very difficult to get them back. It's an insidious cycle.

When I conduct research about new members, I ask questions like, "What is the value of the association for you?" The most common answer is "Well, this is probably my fault, but I don't really know what is available to me and so I haven't participated yet. I keep meaning to set aside an hour or two to scan their website to learn more, but I just haven't found the time." These folks have tuned out the association's emails.

If this issue isn't addressed, these new members get more disengaged over time. Their membership lapses. They might even become word-of-mouth detractors, all because the email campaign of the association sabotages its member onboarding efforts.

Now, it might seem like I'm telling you to not send welcome messages, but that is not the case. I'm advocating for avoiding three common types of welcome emails:

1   The bureaucratic bore (receipts, invoices, login info)

2   The random read (whatever email the rest of the membership is getting at the time)

3   The long list (the bulleted list of every single one of the association's benefits, a favorite-article index, and a catalog of every resource created in the last ten years)

These types of email messages don't work all that well for new members. Let's take a closer look at each kind to see where they go wrong, then we'll explore some better strategies.

The bureaucratic bore

Have you ever noticed that administrative emails, like receipts, that are usually system-generated never look all that nice? Members notice this too.

Carmen quickly scanned the first email, a confusing invoice that wasn't marked paid, even though she'd definitely paid. Then came an email asking her to verify her email address, followed by a separate message to reset her login info. *And why does the receipt email look like it was designed on a dot matrix printer?*

None of these messages are all that engaging, or maybe even necessary. It is possible that your systems are winging off emails to new members that you've never even seen—emails that were written and designed by an IT professional fourteen years ago. (IT professionals, I don't mean any disrespect, because you are technical wizards; feel free to lean on your membership and marketing colleagues to craft the copy.) Stop what you are doing and find those messages. Redesign them, rewrite them, or obliterate the auto-send entirely. If new members can find these documents in their member portal or through a simple link, it might be okay to stop sending them.

The random read

New members are not like all other members. They don't know the association or the names of your benefits, and they might not yet know industry jargon, so any random email the rest of the membership is getting may be confusing or even downright incomprehensible. Many of the emails sent to the membership are promotional in nature and become an anger-inducing upsell for the new member who just opened their wallet to join.

I remember one member saying, "Since I joined all I've gotten is a steady stream of marketing messages. I feel like I spent a pile of money just to be sold to."

When yesterday's email tells you to register for the conference at $750, today's email tries to sell you a $299 research report, and tomorrow's email is shilling webinars for $59 a pop, it's easy to feel that the membership fee didn't really buy you anything. To keep this from happening, some associations hold back all member emails until they've had a chance to send out a few of their new-member onboarding emails.

The long list

Liam opened an email that said, "Welcome, Liam!" His eyes quickly took in paragraph after paragraph of text. He was feeling a little rushed but decided to plow ahead. "You've joined the oldest association in our field. With twelve thousand members worldwide, we are the first place to look for all things about this exciting field. Make sure to explore our vast online library of more than twenty thousand articles. There are 133 on-demand learning modules to increase your knowledge. And make sure you find your local chapter—we have forty-three of them throughout the country." Liam's brain started to glaze over. He scrolled and scrolled (and scrolled some more). There appeared to be a list of benefits, articles, courses to buy, and videos. He clicked a few links. One led him to another list of links on a poorly formatted web page. Clicking on an interesting title brought him to a video that had a one-hour-and-thirteen-minute running time. *Yikes!*

Let's talk about the ubiquitous welcome list of benefits.

When new members encounter a list of benefits, often they can't yet make the connection between your benefits and the solutions they need. So, your benefits list is a bunch of unintelligible words—not very engaging.

"What a minute!" you might be saying. "Don't members join for our benefits?

Nope, they don't! (Weird, isn't it?)

New members join because someone they respect suggested they should. The number-one recruitment channel for most new members is word-of-mouth recommendations. Students join when their professor tells them to. Employees join when their boss recommends the association. People join when they see an industry influencer getting value. Word-of-mouth recommendations are often short. A suggestion to join an association could be as straightforward as "I really enjoy belonging to ABC Association. You might want to check it out."

Based on this simple recommendation from someone they trust, people may scan the association's home page, then join, with *no idea what the benefits are!* They might not even know what the purpose of this association is; heck, they might not even know what associations are.

When a member doesn't know much about the association they just joined, a welcome letter that is a benefits list is indecipherable. Sure, new members know what a newsletter, webinar, or conference is; they just have no idea how any of these things help them personally or can assist the organizations they work for. These things sound like more time, effort, and money. And should they click a link and find an hour-long video, or a fifty-page research report, or a white paper that's a forty-five-minute read, they'll assume everything the association offers will consume their time and mental energy.

Start Off Member Conversations Right

If the usual email lineup doesn't work, what does?

You have three great options here, and feel free to rotate through them in your new-member messaging campaign, because variety is engaging. The three options are:

1 The snack-sized solution
2 The happy hello
3 The leaning-in listen

The snack-sized solution

Your members are time-pressed, just like everyone else. *Time-pressed* is a nice way of saying absolutely, positively, bananas busy. Even though new members are busy, they are usually willing to spend a little time reading a few emails. We don't want to train them to think that every email they receive from us is going to be a twenty-minute commitment. Email as a communication channel generally warrants a less-than-one-minute read per message (unless the content is spectacularly fun or crucial).

For emails to members, especially messages for new members, short-form content is better than long paragraphs and long lists. Try an experiment where you write short messages counted in sentences, not paragraphs. The only goal of these sentences is to entice readers to click to access more information. To be mindful of their time, link to other brief content like a snappy blog post, quick article, one- to three-minute video, infographic, or chart.

A client-friend of mine calls this "snackable content." Like fresh, salty popcorn, this kind of content is light, easy, and interesting. Emails like this demonstrate to new members that reading messages from your association is worthwhile. Think brain candy!

No more lists, no more paragraphs. Say goodbye to three, four, ten embedded links.

I know. I know. This is sooooo hard.

Because it's usually mega difficult to get on the association's weekly email schedule, you want to tell members everything all at once. As you're writing, you think, *Oh yeah, I should just slip in a link for that new product. Our new members will love that.* You're bursting at the seams to let them know about all the cool things you've created for them.

But taking the-more-the-merrier approach to communications backfires, especially with new members. When we make our message too long and too complicated, members will ignore it (and soon us as well).

So, we need to discipline ourselves to choose only one goal, one message, and one quick call to action for each email.

Here's one way to think about new-member communications: each message should solve one tiny problem a new member is likely having right now. This can work well for professional associations whose pipeline of new members is consistent, like those with a strong base of student members the association can convert to core members after graduation. When members achieve predictable milestones, we can develop short, compelling, value-rich communications that, over time, give them a comprehensive tour of how the association can help them. Don't worry about creating a whole big tour right now. Let's start at the beginning.

What types of milestones and changes are coming up for members?

- Have they just graduated and are they now looking for a job?

- Is their organization about to buy (or be bought by) another organization?

- Is a new regulation coming that they need to know about?

- Are they trying to adapt to the culture at a new job?

- Have they recently become a manager of a former peer and they don't know how the heck to deal with that?

What are all the big and little problems new members have? What milestones are they hitting in their careers, organizations, or lives? What experiences are most common right now?

Those of you who work with an industry association, I didn't forget about you! You also have options to set up new-member communications that span professions and are relevant in that moment. You may want to focus on trends in the industry. Is there something going on in the field that is impacting the organizations that new members belong to? Sometimes members join because their organization increased its revenue, moved into a new vertical market, or is now subject to new government regulations. All of these topics are relevant to them.

Identify as many little and big problems as you can and then map them to the bits and bites of snackable content you have sprinkled all over your website. Here's an example of one professional association's new-member welcome email:

> Welcome to [association name]! We are delighted you joined our community. As a new member, you might be wondering what's in store for you. Let's go for a quick one-minute tour.
>
> [An embedded video speaks to one critical problem new members often experience and the association's solution.]
>
> We'll be back in just a couple of days to continue our tour.

Short emails linking to snackable content deliver immediate value into new members' hands, as well as proof they made a great decision in joining the association.

The happy hello

I had a professor, let's call him Dr. Tedious, who would drag an overhead projector from class to class so he could lecture from his thirty-year-old acetate slides about supply chain management.

He would drone on in the driest way possible (think: Sahara Desert) for a solid hour, making eye contact only with his slides. When there were no more slides, the class would abruptly end. Dr. Tedious would straighten up, carefully put his slides into a taped-up cardboard box, unplug the projector, and shuffle from the room, leaving all of us wondering where we could go and hide to catch a few Z's before the next class.

Some professional emails sound like they were written by my long-ago professor. But our messages don't have to sound like passages from a calculus textbook. (Mathematics societies, you might get a pass on this one.)

Think about tone as a continuum.

Best Friend
Forever Tone

Super-
Professional Tone

On one end of the continuum is the Super-Professional Tone. It's polished to perfection, uses big words you have to look up, and is so grammatically correct the copy actually sounds wrong, but you know it's not, because it's as if a steel-spined, mistake-proof English governess wrote it. Many professional member associations communicate in a Super-Professional Tone. This voice is expected and safe but also aloof, perhaps bureaucratic, and institutional-sounding.

At the other end of the continuum, there is the Best Friend Forever, or BFF, Tone. It's friendly, fun, silly, or quirky. I also call this the Happy Dog Tone. Think of the happiest dog you know. What would that pup say to you if they could talk? You don't even have to guess—google "Meet Dug" and watch a video clip from the Pixar movie *Up*. Okay, I'll wait here while you go watch it. It will just take a minute and a half.

Did you watch it?

Are you smiling? Just a little?

That's what the BFF or Happy Dog Tone does. It makes readers smile. And when readers smile, they become more engaged with your message. And when they become more engaged with your message, an opportunity opens up for them to become more engaged members.

I know what you're thinking! You're thinking, *But our members are smart, ultra-professional, wildly successful rocket scientists/climate advocates/leaders of our industry or profession, so wouldn't talking to them as their pretend BFF be a little, um, unprofessional? We can't go around being casual. Our communications must have some gravitas!*

I hear you, but remember I said tone is a continuum? You don't have to swing your messaging suddenly from one side of the continuum to the other. That would confuse members and cost your association some credibility.

But you could move a teensy step on the continuum. You could write like a moderately happy dog and see how that goes. Or you could slip in one happy sentence. Warm up the tone of your emails by a mere quarter of a degree. Even that little bit will have a positive effect. Try moving a speck, and if that goes well, move another speck toward your goal. Maybe within six months or a year, you'll have changed the tone of your messaging enough that you'll see readers engaging more.

Plus, I contend that your mission can be deadly serious, but your messaging doesn't have to be. Forks Over Knives wants more people to switch to plant-based eating in order to radically cut down the number of preventive illnesses in the world, reducing operations like cardiac bypasses, some cancers, and diabetes. An extremely serious mission. But their welcome message says, "Whether you are a veggie-curious omnivore or a lifelong vegan, you are welcome here!" A light, friendly, warm message.

A growing number of professional member associations are starting to test out the BFF Tone. And they're finding it has another advantage I haven't talked about yet.

Remember messaging option #1? The snack-sized solution taught us that short and snappy messaging is more engaging. And now I'm going to contradict myself (a little), because sometimes members will read emails written in the BFF Tone all the way to the end even if the message is a bit longer because they are having such a good time. Or sometimes you need more text to impart a happy tone. (Hmmm, it seems we have a chicken-or-egg scenario here.) What's important to know is that if you're leaning into a happy tone, it's okay to use more words as long as they add up to an engaging read. To give you a taste of what I'm talking about, here's the welcome email from the Virtual Networking Incubator (an event and community I created with Arianna Rehak, CEO of Matchbox Virtual Media, to see if virtual networking could be meaningful, fun, and effective):

> We are delighted that you are a part of the Virtual Networking Incubator!

> We've been poring over the applications, and this is what we have found. We are introverts and extroverts. We work with small and large associations. Our members are very diverse, and our own past networking event experiences are also wonderfully varied. But we all have one thing in common—we are super invested in collaborating to figure out virtual networking.

We are so looking forward to connecting, cocreating, and collaborating with you! You will get more information the morning of the first gathering, so you'll know exactly what to expect and what tools to bring along with you. Until we meet, feel free to roam around the Incubator site and take a look at the resources.

ARIANNA & AMANDA

Stiff and formal writing, while grammatically correct and safe, can be a chore to read. Light, informal, and friendly writing, on the other hand, is a sheer joy to read, even if the message itself is not all that profound. It's as if the words are woven into a warm blanket that makes your brain feel snuggly. Who doesn't like that?

The leaning-in listen

We don't always have to be the ones doing the talking. We can invite our new members to talk to us, and we can let go of any unrealistic expectation that we need to be mind readers! That listening is an option may come as a relief for many association execs, especially those who work with a diverse membership (many trade associations are in this category) or complicated benefits structure. When it's impossible to know exactly what each new member wants and needs in any given moment, we can ask. Does this mean we need to listen to every member individually? Well, it depends.

If your association has a manageable number of new members joining and you have the time and human power, there is a lot of value in calling new members. In the New Member Engagement Study that I cocreated with my partners at Dynamic Benchmarking, we found that staff calls

to members do correlate to increased new-member retention. (You should take a second to download that report. It
is great—if you don't mind me tooting our horn just a bit.)
Some membership and marketing staff make phone calls an
outsized portion of their responsibilities because listening
to members' personal and organizational wants and needs
makes it easier for staff to connect members to the resources
and other members that will help them most.

Here's what the concierge-like service looks like for
one director of member strategy. New members receive an
email encouraging them to sign up for a conversation with
the staff director via her online calendar. Conversations
are scheduled for no more than thirty minutes. During
the call, the director asks the member questions about
their company, role, career, challenges, and goals. In the
last five minutes of the call, she links some of the member's most pressing problems to solutions offered by the
association. The conversation might end like this: "I heard
you say that you're just starting to implement an innovative project. What your company is doing is exciting and
new, and not many members have tried this yet. But I do
know of another company—not a competitor of yours—
that is trying something similar. Would you like me to introduce you?" Or "You mentioned your worries about some
upcoming government regulations. We have a popular podcast, and there's a recent episode that covers just that topic.
I'll send you a link." Less than twenty-four hours later, she'll
send all the resources, data, links, and in a separate email
the introduction she promised.

After two weeks, the director checks in: "Were those
resources helpful? What are you working on now?" Is this
time-consuming? Yes! But for some associations, this sort

of personalized conversation has tremendous ROI. According to the New Member Engagement Study, phone calls rank as the second-most effective new-member engagement tactic behind emails. But phone calls may be nearly impossible if you have an avalanche of new members joining.

Another highly personable and customized strategy some associations use is a new-member listening tour. *Woohoo! Get ready for a road trip, you all! My road-trip playlist is ready to go.* Instead of waiting for members to come to an event, staff go to them. I've heard of CEOs and staff (particularly of state associations) scheduling a bunch of meetings, then jumping into a car for a week so they can talk to new members at their places of employment or over breakfast, lunch, or dinner. While these listening tours tend to pack on the miles (and pounds), everyone I've talked to who's tried it has raved over the results. Not only do new members give positive feedback, but staff members learn a lot too. They hear about new members' wants and needs; they find value being in their members' environment; and they learn what is going on in the profession or industry. The knowledge gained from listening tours can inform innovation, new content, and—yep!—new ways to curate member experiences. Oh, and by the way, listening tours don't have to involve a road trip. Your listening tour can totally happen virtually (but sadly I'm missing those amazingly crispy diner hash-browns already!).

I've been cheerleading phone calls and listening tours, but I realize they are not for every association or every type of member. No worries! There are other ways to have a conversation, which is good news for associations who have hundreds or thousands of new members joining at the same time.

There has been a very pronounced evolution in new-member orientation events. Monthly webinar-style overviews of the association benefits used to be the norm. Now these events tend to be far more interactive. During some, new members are asked to introduce themselves. Others are free-flowing, allowing members' questions and interests to determine the content. Some events are structured as networking or roundtable events, and the organizers pull in different association resources depending on where the conversation goes.

Another strategy that is piquing my interest is what I call the question-tree model, which works well when your member contacts are very diverse. The question-tree model is a mechanism delivered via email, web page, or chat that asks members a series of questions to rapidly determine which resources they need most.

Here's a sample question tree:

Are you most interested in?
- Strategy
- Innovation
- Marketing
- Operations
- Leadership

Let's say they select Innovation. They'd get a follow-up question:

What aspect of innovation would you like to learn about?
- Overcoming resistance
- Change management
- Market intelligence
- Innovation process

Innovation process would direct them to a well-designed landing page with these options:

- Design thinking (with links to a virtual course and a one-minute course trailer)

- Collaborative cocreation (with a link to an ebook on how to design a cocreation event)

- Lean innovation (with a link to the latest article)

Within just a few seconds of using the question-tree method, members could be browsing content and resources on topics they care about. Forced-choice questions are always tricky because the answers may not be what a new member is looking for, so let them know they can click reply and message a real person.

When your new members join and never take another step, it is likely because they are ignoring your emails. Try snack-sized solutions, a happy hello, or the leaning-in listen to engage them in your emails *and* your association.

Harness the Power of Firsts

There is a power in firsts for members. A great first email entices members to read more of your messages. A great first conference lures attendees back for a second great conference. A great first chapter meeting attracts members to the next one.

Many associations tap into the power of firsts. First-time attendees at an event might get a star on their badge or an invite to an orientation or reception. This is an excellent start and I encourage you not to stop there, because as you dive deeper, you'll see there's power in the details—namely the first experience of the first experience.

Say a new member is coming to a conference for the very first time. Their first experience of the conference is probably not the opening-night reception for newcomers. Their first experience might be when they register, receive the first conference email, or walk through the doors to the venue.

The folks at Walt Disney World start your vacation experience long before your trip. The parent who books the vacation gets a series of thoughtfully written emails that heighten anticipation and make planning fun. Upon arriving at the airport after a long trip to Orlando, Disney takes care of luggage and transfers, which is pure magic for parents toting a toddler and a mountain of heavy gear. (BTW, why does a twenty-seven-pound toddler need 550 pounds of strollers, diapers, and supplies? This is today's big philosophical question. You're welcome!)

What amusement park does that? Disney invests in hundreds of experiential first impressions, so that even before your vacation starts, you can't wait to experience the real thing. Disney's Imagineers understand that even the smallest details matter. I still remember arriving at the Polynesian Village Resort as an eight-year-old. Before we entered the hotel, my dad stopped in the dead center of the sidewalk to look off into a garden with awe. He walked a few feet to the left, then to the right, and cocked his head. You see, he noticed there was a subtle thrum of drum music following us. *Where is the speaker?* he wondered. Before long, he located the source: a fake rock designed to blend in with all the real ones in the area. Disney could have hidden speakers under eaves, but no. At Disney World, rocks can ~~sing~~ rock out!

Those rocks knocked my dad's socks off. For the next few days, he marveled over everything from the lack of trash to the flower gardens that were replanted nightly to the way the characters seem to come and go without actually opening a door. Sure, we were all excited about the rides, parades, shows, and fireworks, but Dad's amazement about the logistics captured us all.

We don't all have the nearly unlimited resources of Disney, but we don't need to. We can still leverage the power of firsts.

How do you optimize for firsts? Mentally map out your new member's journey and note all the firsts (think: new-member orientation, free online training course, first time attending the annual conference, etc.). Now that you have a list, what are all the first touchpoints for those first experiences you have with members?

How can you make each experience immediately engaging and exciting? How can you make it easier for members to get value fast?

In the first hours, days, and weeks after they join, members make dozens or hundreds of observations, and all these little bits come together to form an impression. Observations quickly become judgments about the association. These judgments can be very positive or very negative. As association leaders, we have some control over the ultimate verdict!

I can already tell that you are going to be a fantastic Chief Experience Officer! Let's dive into the next stage of our member engagement journey.

2

assess

*"I just make it my business to get along
with people so I can have fun. It's that simple."*

BETTY WHITE

KAT ALMOST spills her orange spice tea when she sees her name in the email's subject line. It's a cold and crisp Tuesday morning, and she has just sat down at her desk. She has exactly thirteen minutes to look through her already jammed inbox before the day's back-to-back meetings start.

"Kat, you were mentioned in a community post," reads the subject line. *Whoa!* thinks Kat. *I just joined. Why am I being mentioned in their online community?* She logs in to read the text: "Let's extend a very warm welcome to this week's new members! Philip, Kat, and Joe, we would love to know more about you and what you're working on, so please do take a few minutes to check out the Introductions area of the forum. We also have a handy Getting Started area that has some tips for how we interact in this community. When you're ready, please introduce yourself and let us know how we can support you. We welcome you!" Kat exhales. *Oh, that wasn't so bad at all. It was kind of nice to be personally welcomed.*

Kat's mind travels back to last week when she attended another organization's professional lunch event. She walked up to two women standing behind the registration desk and was immediately struck by the lack of smiles. In fact, neither spoke to her. One of the women looked especially dour. *Like a disapproving schoolteacher*, Kat thought. She had to say, "Hi, I'm Kat Taylor." The first woman thumbed through the name badges while the second put a program in a bag. Handing Kat her stuff, the second woman pointed and said, "You are over there." Kat had heard that this group was top-notch, but the less-than-tepid greeting dampened her enthusiasm. *Well, this new association certainly seems different from those stodgy lunch buddies from last week*, Kat thinks now.

Kat clicks the Introductions link and skims a few recent posts. She notices a few of these folks work in organizations like hers, at a similar level, on similar projects. *I guess I've never really thought about it, but there are people in other organizations like me*, she muses. This revelation comes as a bit of a surprise because there is certainly no one like her at her current workplace.

Within a few days, Kat notices digest emails coming to her from the association's online community. Most days she skims the headlines. Most of the topics don't apply to her at the moment, but some of them do, and in those cases, she finds it valuable to read the ping-pong between her fellow members.

There is a slightly voyeuristic feeling to reading some of the conversations, a little like peeking behind the curtain. Here in actual print, people are freely expressing feelings about topics she *never* talks about. Not to her direct reports and certainly not to her manager, who doesn't invite personal commentary from Kat or any kind of innovative thinking, for that matter.

Some of the most interesting conversations she's found in the digests are about how to handle human interactions. She lingers over posts with subject lines like "How do I get my team on board with a new mandate from management?" and "Have you ever had a boss who was acting against a policy?" and "What to do when a super productive direct report is hated by peers."

The other members of the community do not seem scared of these topics. Kat can see participants empathizing, helping, and cheering each other on. For a while, Kat watches the conversations with fascination. *Why does everyone feel safe talking about these sensitive topics?* she wonders. *Why is everyone so positive, so kind, and so supportive? It's like each person in the forum is taking care to be overly compassionate. Are their organizations far less cutthroat than mine?*

One of the most active participants, Kat notices, is Susan. After a while, Kat realizes that Susan is on the staff of the association. Susan has a particularly friendly style that makes Kat feel Susan is super approachable, almost like a best friend Kat has yet to meet in person. Susan emphasizes with capitals or bold letters, sometimes even *both* CAPITAL and **bold** letters when something is **REALLY IMPORTANT**. Susan also writes like a fun person talks, with flourishes of emoji, symbols, and memes thrown in. At first, Susan's style seems slightly too exuberant for a professional forum, but soon Kat comes to really enjoy it.

Susan, Kat decides, is the group cheerleader who makes the open exchange of information normal and beneficial. If someone posts on a Friday and no one has responded by Tuesday, Susan notes, "I love this question, Carlos! I can't wait to hear what the group has to say." And responses pour in. When two members get into a tussle in a thread, Susan tries to defuse the situation: "Bill and Sanjay, you both have such great insights on this topic. I was recently talking with another member, and they had another take, which was *X*. I bet there are many ways to come at this; I'd love to hear more wisdom from you and our group." Susan even starts threads. "Hey everyone," she posts one day, "I've been hearing that *Y* might be a new trend. What do you think? Is this a thing?"

One day Kat was reading a post that included the unfamiliar acronym TOS. She tried to infer the meaning once more from the context, but she was still puzzled. Rather than take the time to look it up, she continued scrolling the thread. Not too far down was a message from Susan: "Popping in here really quick to note that TOS = Terms of Service." *Ah! Now it all makes sense!*

Susan's demeanor isn't unusual in the association. The people who write the newsletters, host the programming, and send emails have the same warmhearted spirit. Their attitude is motivating but not invasive.

Mostly the forum is populated by people like Kat. People seem to fall over each other to respond. Experienced people help those who are new. Folks who have successfully completed a big project help others who are starting their big project. Peers work with colleagues to think through thorny issues. Sometimes they exchange great resources.

The more Kat reads, the more she feels like she has found her community.

· · · · ·

ONCE MEMBERS learn that the association's emails are valuable and maybe even fun, they start reading many of the messages the association sends, which opens up all sorts of opportunities for connection.

The split-second observations they make as they start hanging out in online forums or attending events lead to assessments about whether the people who make up the community are their kind of people. In these early stages, they're asking themselves, *Does this community have a vibe that feels right to me?*

Everyone has had some sort of group experience. In many groups, there is a good dynamic, like in a close-knit group of friends who make each other laugh so hard tears stream down their faces. Or in a neighborhood where all the residents share tools and fix each other's lawn mowers. Or in a work team that magically bonds over a gnarly project that seemed like it would never end.

Nearly everyone has also experienced a bad group dynamic. Maybe a community of parents of school-aged kids became overly political and a little bit backstabby. Or at university, there were group projects where one person didn't do their fair share. Or the memory of being hurt by a high school clique's malicious gossip still stings.

With good and bad group dynamics from the past coloring people's thoughts, they compare their new-member experiences with the other experiences they have had.

When people try to join a new community, they make the "Are these my kind of people?" assessment very quickly. We can sniff out telltale undesirable behaviors in a fraction of a second. Our amygdala tells our legs to start running the moment there's even the slightest hint of a bad group dynamic we have experienced in the past. So, associations must convince new members that this is a good group, fast. The good news is there's a lot we can do to help newcomers make a positive assessment of the association community.

Warm Up Your Welcome
. . . .

There was a time when public speaking made me weak in the knees, literally. I didn't really want to go to my first Toastmasters meeting, but I knew I had to. I had decided that no matter what, I was going to get better at public speaking! *Dammit!* I wanted to actually sleep the night before a presentation, and I wanted to obliterate the horrible swarm of butterflies that would swoop inside my belly before a talk. No matter how difficult or painful the process, I decided I was going to do it.

Imagine my surprise that the meetings were not at all difficult or painful. I was warmly greeted the moment I walked through the door by a woman about my age. We chatted while she showed me the juice and bagel table, then she found me a seat and introduced me to the people sitting on either side of me. My new neighbors asked what brought me to Toastmasters; they shared their speaking goals; and they asked about mine.

Before I knew it, the meeting was underway. The host of the meeting said just a few opening words and called on me to stand and quickly introduce myself. The intro wasn't too hard, because after all I knew the subject matter well—the subject was me! As I concluded my two-sentence introduction, I was surprised by the sound of applause and the big smiles directed at me from around the room.

Warm welcomes benefit everyone. Most of the engaged members I talk to have fond memories of their warm welcomes too.

Warm welcomes are usually one of the first signals to new members that this community is filled with people like them. The registration desk at a chapter meeting or conference is an obvious place to offer a warm welcome. This is a great time to act like you're on a stakeout: What is actually happening at the registration desk? Is it a warm welcome or is it an administrative transaction? Because the goal is to get their name tag into their hands, right? But what seems like a simple transaction to you means the world to them. Remember that new members and attendees are like strangers coming to a party where they don't know anyone. That feeling of being a newcomer can be downright terrifying.

The warmer your welcome, and the more you can put them at ease, the better. When attendance is light, you might have time to talk with each attendee, but when your event scales, you might need reinforcements. Some event planners station welcomers around the registration area to pitch in when the throng comes, and to identify people they've never seen before and take time to talk with them. I've seen these designated welcomers escort members into the meeting room, pointing out coat racks and bathrooms and the refreshments table along the way, and then introduce them to someone else before returning to their post at the desk.

Designating welcomers also helps keep longtime friends from circling up. New members can spot cliques from miles away. Walking into a room where everyone is talking and laughing in a tight circle at the front of the room is the worst experience. The first-time attendee thinks, *This is so awkward! Do I try to join in? No, they seem like they all know each other. What the heck are they talking about anyway? I guess I'll just slink over to a seat and pretend I'm not eavesdropping. I hate this.* Perhaps make a pact with your board to focus on welcoming members at chapter meetings and to find other times when longtime friends and colleagues can meet.

Warm welcomes can happen at other times and places too. Members remember the warm welcomes they received during a new-member orientation call, webinar, or reception. Warm welcomes happen in person and in the virtual space, at events or asynchronously. They can happen at conferences, training, chapter events, or via email, video, or phone. Warm welcomes can come from staff, board members, committee members, or fellow members. The warmer the welcome, the better, and many warm welcomes are better than none.

Offer Social Proof
. . . .

Another strategy that lets members know that the association is full of people like them is to show them: offer social proof.

Social proof may have been invented in the consumer marketing world, in the form of likes, reviews, and follows, but social proof is also a powerful strategy for associations seeking to engage new members. How do associations use social proof in a genuine, non-sleezy way to help new members see there are others like them?

A photo collage of real members can be useful. Don't only post photos of your board members because they are easy to photograph at a meeting. Board members tend not to be very representative of the entire membership. Make sure you represent the diversity of your membership within your photo collage. This photo collage can be displayed on your home page, registration page, or application brochure.

Photo collages of members can work for trade associations as well as professional associations, and you might also try a logo collage of member organizations so that prospective and new members can see that people from partner, peer, and competitive organizations have joined. There are all sorts of collage variants. You could display a leaderboard of annual conference registrants. Or you could include a list of that week's new and renewing members on your home page and in your e-newsletter if renewals happen year-round. This shows everyone that the association is healthy; new members are joining all the time.

I've seen some delightful trailers for annual conferences that tick all the social-proof boxes. While the camera might be pointed at a celebrity or industry-famous speaker most of the time, it also pans the audience. In a two-second clip, new and prospective members might see others who look like them and who appear to be having fun. Trailers can be used for virtual events, courses, certification, and even for other benefits such as the online forum.

Well-crafted video testimonials also offer social proof. Testimonials take the pressure off the association to sell membership, benefits, and events, because members do it for you in their own words. Here are some questions you can ask members, attendees, and volunteers in order to craft a testimonial:

- What do you think of the [membership/event/product/resource]?

- How did the [membership/event/product/resource] help you?

- What do most like about the [membership/event/product/resource]?

- How are you using the [membership/event/product/resource]?

If you have an active online community, make sure a daily or weekly digest is sent to all new members by default. Seeing thoughts, questions, and solutions from their peers is valuable for new members and offers social proof. *Oh, look at that thread, there are three members talking about an issue that I've been interested in for a long time. I very much agree with the direction Asha is headed in.*

Another way to leverage social proof is to recruit members from a targeted segment to partner with you during an event for that same targeted subset of new members. Let's say you're running an orientation meeting for new members who have recently graduated from college. You could recruit an engaged young professional to cohost, present, answer questions, or moderate the chat—whatever role is comfortable to them. Seeing someone who is a step ahead of them leading the conversation is motivating and gives newcomers the sense that there are people like them in the community.

Think about all the ways you can show new members that there are many people like them in the association.

Explain Your Jargon

During every point of contact members have with the association, we want them to sense that they are insiders. But sometimes, accidentally, they'll have an experience that makes them feel like an outsider. Jargon and other excluding words can have this effect.

SEO, advertorial, CTA, and *list hygiene* are all terms you can find in the unofficial dictionary of marketing speak. My fellow marketers like to throw the newest, shiniest words into conversation (and I'm guilty of this sometimes too). Marketers are not alone in creating their own language. I know this because my electrical-engineer husband spends all day shouting acronyms and technical words into the phone: "We don't even have a specification for that MAC." "What about the DCS?" I just heard this gem wafting up from downstairs: "The analyzer communicates with PROFIBUS." I know about school buses and city buses, but PROFIBUS? It sometimes sounds like an alien has co-opted his brain. Since market- ers and engineers come from two totally different planets, I don't feel bad about not knowing his language, or he mine, but if he were a professional colleague, it would be different.

A unique language develops in every industry, profession, and field. These new words, phrases, and acronyms become shorthand for the professionals in that industry. They are a quick way of describing something that would otherwise take a whole sentence or paragraph or white paper to explain. Jargon is also a signaling device. Using these words is a way of demonstrating you are knowledgeable, up-to-date, and in the know. Understanding the language is a badge that shows you are part of the community.

But what if a new member doesn't yet know the lan- guage? Not knowing the language is like a flashing neon sign that says "You Are an Outsider!" (Even though at some point we all had to learn what this invented business lan- guage meant.)

Our goal is to help our new members, who are probably feeling a little unsure and out of place, become insiders, part of our community. Instead of letting industry jargon alienate your new members, use it for good. Teach the words of your community to new professionals. Carefully select a word or phrase and use it in context, define it, and maybe even give some descriptive examples in the content you provide.

When your new members move into the next stage, Participation, they will hit the ground running.

Like jargon, there are other words and phrases that can repel new members from the community, most notably non-inclusive language. So many associations are striving to be highly inclusive, and we can demonstrate our intention with language. Double-check your messaging for language that may unintentionally exclude, stigmatize, or offend someone. Have you read *The Dictionary of Lost Words* by Pip Williams? It really woke me up to the fact that words have histories, and some of those histories are pretty terrible. Through the generations, we forget the original meanings of words and phrases. When in doubt, become a detective to make sure you stay clear of expressions that have a history of sexist, racist, ageist, or similarly othering connotations. A simple Google search can give you much more information about conscious and inclusive language resources.

Members love it when you get their name right. Feel free when introducing a sponsor or speaker to ask how they pronounce their name. Feel free to also ask them what pronouns they prefer. Many associations are updating the required fields on application and registration forms, eliminating some (like the field for titles like Mr. and Mrs.) and adding others (like a field for preferred pronouns like he/him, she/her, and they/them).

As many associations grow into global organizations, it's also important to consider how language shows preference to the association's home country—for example, referencing seasons leaves an entire hemisphere out. Avoid common phrases like "Christmas holiday" in favor of "December break."

Consider Culture Cues

Newcomers to the association also determine if other members of the group are like them by picking up on culture cues.

Culture cues are the telling behaviors, rituals, and quirks of the group. Some cultures evolve organically, and some are nudged in a certain direction. Many cultures have a mix of positive and negative aspects. New members notice *everything*.

Association leaders can amplify and encourage the positive aspects to mold the culture so that it becomes beneficial for members. Sometimes a member culture is so entrenched, it is hard to change. But you can make headway a bit at a time. Here's how.

Before members get together for a virtual event, in-person meeting, mentoring session, or any kind of interaction, think about what kind of culture you want to create. Do you want a community that's friendly, enthusiastic, caring, and generous? Pick your own adjectives for your specific member community.

With your adjectives in mind, try to exhibit these qualities in all the communications you send to members. Alter the tone and choose colors and graphics that allow you to communicate in the way you hope members will communicate with each other.

While developing the Virtual Networking Incubator, we wanted to create a virtual lab-like community where participants could feel safe adding knowledge even if in the moment their idea felt silly. Super-silly ideas are sometimes the breakthrough a group needs! Working backward from our desired behaviors, we decided that we wanted a community that was open, generous, friendly, caring, and kind. We hoped that our communications would set the tone.

Here's an excerpt from an early email:

> The *enthusiasm* you brought to our first gathering together was *AWESOME*! Your chat was so upbeat and supportive. You can't see it, but right now we are doing jazz hands because we are so happy!
>
> Two weeks until our next gathering seems like a long time, so if you have time to play, we've set up a place to connect during the days in between. *Remember to mark your calendars for our next meeting.* Expect more fast-paced fun, perhaps with a dash of hilarious tech snafus on our part (things like that just happen during virtual events, right?).
>
> We can't wait to see you at the second gathering!
>
> ARIANNA & AMANDA

While drafting each email, we tried to communicate our own enthusiasm for upcoming events and our budding, heartfelt appreciation for the participants' willingness to try something new with us.

Signaling these culture cues helped because the 150 participants who joined us were enthusiastically ready to pitch in and work with each other.

Cultivate a Sense of Belonging

Ideally, associations become a professional home for members, a place to gather and to be motivated, supported, and energized. Having the opportunity to meet and talk with like-minded people is invaluable, especially when members are open and sharing.

This is especially important when members feel very alone, even isolated, at their workplaces. A common refrain I hear from members is "I'm the only person in my organization who does what I do." Maybe they're the only controller, programmer, or social media specialist. The work is so specialized that in their organization, it's not understood or valued, and they feel ostracized. Or maybe they're the only person at a particular level. Their boss doesn't get them, and they can't confide in their direct reports. Or a member might feel alone because she's the only woman in an organization dominated by men, or they're a parent of young children, which means they can't work late at night or go out after work to socialize. Maybe they feel isolated because of racial, religious, age, or other differences from their colleagues.

When professionals can't connect with other like-minded folks, their feelings of isolation intensify. They may feel discouraged, frustrated, or like an imposter. Left unchecked, those feelings may start to balloon until that person wants to leave the profession, industry, or field. Being different from everyone else can change your career trajectory, foster feelings of unfairness, and be demotivating.

For those who stay in their profession, the association can be a lifeline. When you have the pervasive feeling that you can't turn to your coworkers, it's comforting to belong to an association that's filled with people just like you. At the annual conference, you can get together to refill the motivational tanks. At chapter meetings, you can swap war stories, remind each other why you do this work, and cheer each other on.

One association that serves a very male-dominated industry has formed a women's alliance. Many of these women work in all-male departments for male supervisors who tend to either overlook their contributions or in some cases, overtly disparage it. The members of the women's alliance find that telling stories and supporting each other is cathartic, and they have founded an underground movement with the goal of growing women's participation in the industry. Instead of becoming angry and dropping out, more women are staying in their careers, having a bigger voice in critical issues, and attracting more female applicants to their companies and industry.

Associations can create a welcoming space for members to connect with each other. When members feel like they have found their community, they may be ready to explore the next stage of the member journey.

3

participate

"Takin' on a challenge is a lot like riding a horse. If you're comfortable while you're doin' it, you're probably doin' it wrong."

TED LASSO

"HELLO, KAT! Great to see you here," Kat reads in the virtual event's chat. *Oh wow! Here they are again welcoming people by name*, she thinks. The host is a bubbly, smiling woman named Rhonda, and she has a partner, Emily, and both are chatting like crazy—Rhonda, verbally, and Emily, in the chat box.

Normally, Kat multitasks during webinars, but today she pushes her phone away. She then flips it face down for good measure. Kat figures she can get back to her email if, after a few minutes, the event doesn't pay off.

But pay off it does! Instead of launching into a slide deck, the host starts asking questions. The first question is super easy to answer: dark chocolate! *No contest—dark chocolate is yards, miles, universes better than white chocolate! Is white chocolate technically even chocolate?*

The next question makes her pause: "What has you most optimistic today?" Today has been a bit of a grind, but if she has to pick one thing, it's that beast of a project she's working on. Sure, it is hard, but she is learning a lot, and if it works, so many possibilities will open to her and the company. Kat starts typing.

"I'd love to know more about your project," says Ben, another attendee. "Me too," says Laura. "It sounds like I might be working on a similar project," types Mia. "We should chat." Kat feels like she's been toiling away on this project in a deep, dark lonely cave so she loves the idea of connecting with Mia and the other attendees. She feels gratified that her contribution to the chat was popular.

Over the next twenty-five minutes, the host asks them a lot of questions about their organizations, goals, projects, and work. Many of the other new members are interested in the same things she is interested in. And she can tell from the quips and jokes in the chat that they are all just as time-pressed and stressed as she is.

Occasionally, the host screen-shares to show them something new, like how to log in to and navigate the online community, or how to get access to benchmarking data. Kat takes some notes because many of the resources look like they might save her some time in the long run.

One conversation in the chat catches Kat's eye. Another attendee, Richard, seems to be having a tough time following along. His first comment is a little gruff: "This stuff is hard to access! Will you just tell me how to get to that survey?!" Kat thinks, *Uh-oh!* She remembers a few times when Stan, a department vp, made a ruckus because he couldn't get his tech to work and unpleasantly derailed many a meeting. But Emily is right on it. "Sure, Richard, I'm happy to help! All of our surveys are located in the top navigation bar under Resources, and here's the link to that particular survey so you can click and go right there." Richard's chat is quiet for a moment and then: "Now it says I need a password. I don't remember my password! Why do I always have to keep logging in? By the time I get to this survey, I'm going to be ten minutes behind everybody else." Emily doesn't waste any time. "No problem, Richard. I'm going to direct-message you and we'll sort this out very quickly.

And don't worry about missing the group conversation, we're recording it so you can pop back in later if you'd like."

Even though Richard seems a tad grumpy, Kat likes the way Emily leapt in to help him out and didn't let his negativity put a damper on the session.

By the time the orientation webinar winds down, Kat has about fifteen browser tabs open and is excited to dive into some of the articles and resources she's found. She sends a LinkedIn invite to Mia.

As everyone signs off with big smiles and waves, Kat smiles too.

. . . . .

ONCE MEMBERS observe and assess—in other words, get the lay of the land—they might decide they are ready to participate. Participation is a usually a casual exchange, like having a conversation with peers, answering a question in a chat, or voting by raising their hand. Participation can happen organically, but many members never move past the Observe and Assess stages of the member journey. They never feel motivated to participate, and this is too bad because participating and the stages that come after it are where the real engagement magic happens. To get over that hurdle, new members often need a little friendly nudge. I call this priming them to participate.

Prime Members to Participate

Have you ever gone to a meeting where you felt a little uncomfortable? Maybe the other people present were far more senior than you. Maybe you didn't know anyone else. Maybe you came to the project late and didn't know much about it. Maybe you decided to get the lay of the land before jumping in with your ideas. So, you stayed quiet. As time passed, it became harder and harder to say anything at all. At the end, you gloomily left the meeting, mentally kicking yourself for not sharing your great ideas.

This dynamic happens often to members too. When a speaker, trainer, or facilitator reaches the end of their spiel and asks for questions, the room can sometimes be uncomfortably silent. Silence is awkward.

Participation, on the other hand, is engaging and we want lots of it.

One of the best ways to generate a lot of participation is to prime members for participation. When we get members and attendees participating immediately, they'll likely keep participating. The key is nudging them to participate early and effortlessly.

When I'm facilitating a highly interactive session, I nix the usual introduction and start interacting with participants within the first twenty to sixty seconds. I try to make my opening question unexpected to grab their attention, as well as easy and fun to answer so they want to participate. With a nod or a few typed words, attendees make the shift from a passive audience to active participants.

There are many ways to prime members to participate. The warm welcomes that we talked about in the last chapter open the door. Rolling out the red carpet for early birds, thoughtfully breaking the ice, and employing progressive participation techniques can each tamp down normal tentativeness, so people feel comfortable donning their creative caps, rolling up their sleeves, and joining the gang. Let's dive into the details!

Greet your early birds

You've got early birds, right? Early birds are your attend-ees who arrive or log in three, five, or even twenty minutes before the show. Habitual early birds are conscientious folks. They heartily believe that if you're not five minutes early, you're five minutes late! (And they hate being late, believe you me.) Early birding works well for them because it gives them time to feel comfortable in a new space. Before vir-tual events, they want to make sure the tech works. Before in-person events, they might arrive early to escape from the hallway conversations or grab a good seat.

Not always but often, these folks tend toward the intro-vert side of the scale and benefit greatly from our efforts to prime them to participate.

Whether the event is in person or online, I've always been a fan of rewarding the early birds for their punctuality. A reward is a confirmation that the early birds have made a good choice in arriving a few minutes early, and it might convince the latecomers to start arriving a bit earlier too. Latecomers are attendees who log in five, ten, twenty minutes late, missing the welcome and instructions, so they usually feel a little lost for the duration of the event.

So, how do you reward participants for punctuality? One of my favorite strategies is to create an unofficial start game or activity for every event. (I heard this idea first from my colleague Mark Collard at playmeo, a searchable database of games, activities, and icebreakers for any kind of gathering.)

Unofficial starts can be very informal, with the speaker welcoming and chatting with everyone as they enter the physical or virtual room. Unofficial starts can also be highly prescriptive, with rules and a goal. It helps to think about both the purpose of the session and how you want attendees to feel during it. Build your unofficial start with those two things in mind.

Here is one idea for an unofficial start for an online event in Zoom Meetings. (This doesn't work in Zoom Webinar, and yep! I found this out the hard way!)

1   Three to four minutes before the official start time, let your early birds into the meeting.

2   Give them instructions for how to use the Annotate tool.

3   Share your screen with a coloring page or blank screen.

4   Give them a goal: "Color this picture" or "Work together to illustrate this image [of, for example, a garden, a city, a landscape]."

5   While they're at it, play some upbeat royalty-free tunes to set the mood.

6   Be amazed at what they create together.

The virtual-event world is not the only domain for unofficial starts. In physical spaces, you can create fun, easy, inspiring activities that everyone can participate in. Try asking participants to write or draw something or answer a poll via mobile. If you want, you can relate the activity to the topics coming up later. Would you like your participants to collaborate during the session? Have them collaborate during the unofficial start. Will they need to be creative? Propose a creative unofficial start.

Unofficial starts diminish hesitancy during the session itself, so participants can jump right into participating. Think about how you can pull them out of their world, with all its distractions, and into the world you are trying to create during the event.

Break the ice

Unofficial starts are a fun way to increase energy and engagement before kicking off a session's agenda, but some schedules don't allow the time. Not all is lost because you can start any session with icebreakers.

Yep! At the risk of social ostracization, I'm going to extol the virtues of icebreakers. Does the term *icebreaker* set your teeth on edge? You're not alone! Next to rubbery conference chicken, icebreakers are the most maligned meeting tactic. This is too bad because icebreakers, as a concept, are fabulous. It's just that the implementation is generally utterly, totally terrible. Here is a sampling of recent icebreakers I've observed:

- "What's the weather like where you are?" *A tad boring.*

- "Where are you from?" *Too expected.*

- "Share a story that relates to the theme of today's meeting." *Too complicated!*

- "Tell us about a time when you felt really vulnerable." *Too personal, too soon.*

Can you recall one or two icebreaker exercises you were forced to participate in that inspired an *Oh crap, I really don't want to do this* reaction?

Most icebreakers backfire. Most icebreakers make participants feel silly, awkward, embarrassed, and not smart enough, possibly because the host hasn't mapped the icebreaker's outcome with the goal of the meeting. Icebreakers are often thrown in as an afterthought. Icebreakers are thought of as a nice-to-do activity, not a strategic imperative, but they can be a useful tool for setting the stage.

Wouldn't it be great if your icebreakers made participants feel joyful, connected, valued, and excited to participate?

They can!

But first you should know about the strategy of icebreakers. Icebreakers, like most member firsts, are signaling tools. Participants use the icebreaker experience to determine what level of participation is expected of them, whether to tune in or let their minds wander, and whether or not the meeting is going to live up to the promotional hype.

Icebreakers set the stage for what participants will be doing for the next few hours or days. If you want them to have fun during the event, plan a fun icebreaker. If you've planned a meeting around a super meaningful topic, signal this with a thoughtful opening question. The icebreaker will put participants in the right mindset for all that follows.

Speaking of mindsets, one of the enemies of conferences and meetings is all the interruptions and to-dos participants have in their professional life. Phone calls, emails, and texts pull attendees out of the conference and back into their day-to-day. Icebreakers can draw participants' attention back into the meeting world that you have created for them.

What makes for a great icebreaker? Here are some rules. Icebreakers should:

- Catch participants' attention
- Evoke a bit of emotion
- Align with the meeting's theme
- Be doable for everyone
- Require only an itsy-bitsy amount of time and energy

To cue up one particularly creative session, I asked this icebreaker question: "Would you like to be a dragon or have a dragon?" The chat exploded! Here are a few of my favorite responses:

- "The ability to fly would be amazing. And I could toast marshmallows."
- "If I'm a dragon, can I still speak human, or do I only speak Dragonese now? I don't want to be lonely."
- "Imagine the food bills!"

Somewhere in my travels, I heard this question posed and it went right into my Greatest Icebreakers of All Time (GIOAT) list. Here are a few more icebreaker questions from the GIOAT list:

- Is a hot dog a sandwich?
- What kind of car are you today?

- What is your favorite color jelly bean and why?

- What is the most unusual job you've ever had?

- What has you feeling most optimistic these days?

- What is one great piece of advice that you've received?

- If you could have any superpower, what would it be?

- What book, podcast, or movie do you most like to recommend?

- What would the world look like if humans didn't have to sleep?

- If you could choose to be an animal, what would you be and why?

- If money weren't a worry for you, how would you spend your days?

- If you could only eat one food for the rest of your life, what would it be?

- What is something you came across recently that gave you hope or inspiration?

Hopefully, these examples give you a sense of the possibilities. Remember that icebreakers work best when they amplify the theme of your meeting, so pick one or create an opening question that effortlessly segues into your topic.

One last tip for creating effective icebreakers is to vet each idea to make sure that possible answers to the question cast participants in the best light. Try to steer away from questions that might elicit braggy, insensitive, or vulnerable off-the-cuff answers, which participants might regret later.

Answers come in quicker for easy questions ("What is your favorite pizza topping?") than for more thought-provoking questions ("What is something no one else knows about you?"). Pick questions with low stakes and where the group's answers might roughly be divided ("Do you like beach or mountain vacations?"). When in doubt, choose a light, sunny, slightly silly, or funny icebreaker to delight participants.

Get creative with your icebreakers because they are one of the most important parts of any session, especially when you're aiming for lots and lots of participation.

Try progressive participation

One time I attended an educational session with thirteen other people. The trainer asked us to stand in a circle at the back of the room. Our task was to introduce ourselves in a few sentences and pick the person to go next, but not before we repeated all the names and introductions of everyone who had gone before us *in order*.

Everyone seemed to hold it together well, but I was next to last and, as hard as I tried, I forgot some names and jumbled the order. Poof, it felt like all my credibility went up in flames.

Participants trust the person on stage, so when the presenter asks them to perform an overly difficult or complex activity, participants will gamely try. Even if it seems like the activity is working, some participants might secretly feel frustrated, angry, or embarrassed.

As Brené Brown says, "Shame is that warm feeling that washes over us, making us feel small, flawed, and never good enough." These feelings are the ingredients for a toxic cocktail that prevents an attendee from participating with joy, curiosity, or generosity.

When you plan the flow of your event's schedule, cue up topics, early on, that everyone can respond to; ask questions that have no right or wrong answers. Start with questions that will prompt attendees to give quick answers, maybe a word or short phrase.

In person, you might ask for a nod first and then a show of hands. You can ask them to write a word or a little doodle on a sheet of paper and hold it up. During a presentation with leaders from the National Business Aviation Association, we had participants write on paper airplanes and fly their questions to us.

Here, social proof at the front end of your event works in your favor because seeing lots of participation further primes attendees to participate. Start your program with the easiest asks before you transition into activities that require more effort.

Priming for participation and trying progressive participation are strategies that can be expanded anywhere you are looking for member participation. Community managers can adapt these processes to online communities. Editorial staff could use these ideas to seed questions in an article's comment section. Marketing staff can prime members to participate on the association's social media channels.

Whether you are trying to build participation at an event, in your online community, or anywhere members can comment or post, they won't want to participate unless they feel extremely safe.

Make Participation Safe
. . . .

I come from a long line of exceptionally reserved huggers and huggees. Hugging, according to my ancestors, is appropriate only in the following situation: your beloved crashes sideways off a twenty-foot-tall ski jump and survives, and the relief you feel makes you forget yourself. Even then, you make sure there is mutual consent before initiating a restrained hug. If you are feeling particularly overcome, you may execute a single, quick, awkward back pat. These anti-hug tendencies caused some problems early in my career when I worked in one very huggy community. Every time someone would haul off and hug me, I had to fight the urge to adopt an Emperor Kuzco–style defensive kung fu move and yell, "NO TOUCHY!!!" (If you haven't seen *The Emperor's New Groove*, it's a hilarious animated movie, and Yzma might be my favorite villain of all time.)

All communities have a culture and norms. Left unchecked, negative behaviors can flourish. Now, I'm not saying that hugging is necessarily a negative behavior (although asking before hugging is a good idea, no matter how huggy a culture is). This was my own foible, one that I've thankfully overcome (mostly). But there are lots of other behaviors that communities adopt that destroy feelings of safety for other members.

Let's consider online communities, because this is where it is easiest for us to see member culture manifest publicly. When an online community is not actively managed, there are a few behavior types that emerge. On the positive side:

- **The generous benefactor:** These folks monitor the conversation, and when they have something to add, they'll jump in with thoughts and experiences.

- **The connector:** These people look for every opportunity to expand their network and use it for good by making introductions between like-minded people.

- **The cheerleader:** Cheerleaders jump on threads to voice their appreciation. You'll see them say things like "Good point," "So helpful," or "This is interesting, and I'm eagerly following this discussion."

We want more of these behaviors in our communities. But there are also some negative behaviors that can creep in over time:

- **The unappointed police officer:** These people monitor the conversation and slither in with a shaming response whenever they see a real or perceived infraction of the community's written or assumed policy.

- **The flagrant salesperson:** They pounce on any slightly related thread to hard-sell their products or services. You can see their contribution a mile away.

- **The political animal:** These people stir the pot. Instead of having a private candid conversation with staff, they use the forum to publicly complain about the association's policies, procedures, pricing, and people.

Have you seen these personality types in your community?

Perhaps you've experienced some other negative behaviors, like bullying. At events, there can be overtalking or interrupting, and cliquishness. Any of these individual or group behaviors can compromise feelings of safety.

Cultivating a sense of safety is important for all member communities because when members feel safe, they reciprocate with generosity, openness, and kindness. These behaviors, in turn, facilitate the exchange of ideas, offers to help each other, and invitations to connect.

There are a bunch of ways to promote feelings of safety, and we're going to look at a few in detail: managing manners (you may be more familiar with the term *ground rules*, but I advocate for tossing that term out), modeling behaviors you want to see, and addressing bad actors.

Manage manners

You can set the stage with a code of conduct, but I like flipping the idea of a code of conduct on its head. Many codes of conduct are loaded with negative, legalese-infused, heavy-handed copy that can dampen the positive feelings of possibility we wish for our members. And who reads the code of conduct anyway?

For the Virtual Networking Incubator, we decided to take a different approach. We wrote one stanza of our version of a code of conduct that we called the "Golden Rule Haiku":

Learn. Share. Try. Be kind.
Support all. Be generous.
Be here with purpose.

It was a good start, but we wanted to cover more ground, so we asked the Incubator participants if they could develop more verses to inspire the kind of culture we all wanted to participate in. Here's what we got:

Learn. Share. Try. Be kind.
Support all. Be generous.
Be here with purpose.

Do what works for you.
Acknowledge differences.
Show up. Plan to grow.

Look beyond today.
Together we discover.
Creatively play! ☺

The "Golden Rule Haiku" was so short and sweet we could all recite it aloud together at the start of every event.

Not only can a reverse code of conduct inspire positive behaviors, but developing positive rules of engagement can also challenge participants to try on new behaviors, such as:

- **Complimenting others' contributions:** "Boost someone else's idea before adding your own new idea to the conversation."

- **Building on previous ideas and then adding your own:** "Wherever possible, introduce new ideas with the words 'yes, and . . .'"

- **Freeing participants to think more openly:** "Our job here today is only to think about possibilities, which can be silly, fun, or even highly improbable. The wackier, the better!"

Reverse codes of conduct (or golden rule haikus) can be helpful culture cues to new members and are also tangible statements the group can use as reminders if things get out of hand.

Model behaviors you want to see

Participation is a learned behavior and so is additive participation—the good kind of participation that inspires more participation. Not all participation is equal: there is detracting participation, too, in which we see bad behavior. In some cases, you can head off bad behavior by demonstrating how to act.

In professional communities, almost no one sets out to become the misbehaving gremlin (except maybe the rare sociopath). We find that most new members, who want to be successful in the community, are quickly trying to understand the group's norms. Some members will read the rules and etiquette guidelines or the code of conduct, but most won't. Instead, members take cues from other participants. They note the tone, type, and quality of the questions and answers. Subconsciously, they are assessing whether it is safe to be in the community. Are question askers made to feel stupid? If there is disagreement, are respondents shamed in some way?

Moderators can get right in there to demonstrate the kind of behavior they are looking for. (And if your forum, event, or social media presence is too big to moderate with staff, consider training up volunteer ambassadors who can also model the behaviors that make the community better.) For newcomers, it's a relief when leaders model behavior because it gives them reliable reference points. They think:

- *She is really friendly. Okay, I'll be really friendly too.*

- *Oh, look at him saying, "Yes, and . . ." I'll make sure to be additive in my comments!*

- *Hmmm, this is decidedly not a salesy environment. I'll add value and refrain from any hard sells.*

I'm a member of a professional community with a great moderator. She chimes in on many of the threads and is sure to leave a little question or comment for new members or for members we haven't heard from in a while. To one new member, she said, "Great to see you diving right in and asking for help." To a recently absent member, she said, "I'm so glad to see you posting here." She tags others in the community for their good insights: "@Miguel and @Sarah, can you help Marge with her question?" She keeps interesting conversations going with well-placed questions: "What does this mean for your company?" Her tone is always warm, and she has a way of sprinkling in just the right emoji.

I have never seen any bad actors in this community, but if there were some, I trust that she wouldn't turn a blind eye to them.

We'll talk about how to address bad behaviors in the next section, but first I want to note that online forums aren't the only place where modeling matters, and staff are not the only leaders modeling behaviors. Members follow the lead of trainers, speakers, and facilitators who may not be on the staff. Feel free to tell speakers and facilitators what your desired member culture is like, and ask them to imbue that vibe into their behavior.

Members watch board leaders as well. I remember a conversation with one super engaged first-year member—we'll call her Naomi. When she was new to the industry, a family emergency prevented someone in her organization from attending the annual conference. After a couple whirlwind days of making plans and packing, Naomi found herself flying to Seattle in her colleague's place.

While Naomi was standing in the registration line, she noticed a board member (let's call her Joan) roaming around the room exchanging pleasantries with other attendees. Joan started to chat with Naomi about her role and career aspirations and why Naomi had picked this industry. Naomi was amazed and impressed that someone so high up in the association and advanced in her career would make the time to talk to someone so green.

That broke the ice for Naomi. She spent the rest of the conference behaving in an unusually extroverted way, which other attendees responded favorably to. Naomi met a handful of peers, some of whom she remains in close contact today.

Not every board member is like Joan. Sometimes board leaders unintentionally send signals of aloofness, cliquishness, or conceitedness.

Perhaps your board could be a part of the conversation around member culture and behaviors modeling. Have them brainstorm what member culture at your association might look like at its best, and see if they would be willing to take one step that could move the culture in the right direction. Come back to this conversation often.

Address bad actors

There are stories of *that member* in just about every association—the one in fourteen thousand who behaves like a bully but manages to stay within the gray area of the code of conduct. While I have had firsthand experience experimenting with many of the recommendations in this book, I haven't had to address bad actors yet. But I do know that ignoring their bad behavior destroys feelings of safety for all members.

Associations have seen board members resign because of bad actors. Longtime members fail to renew because of bad actors. Hundreds of people silently refrain from contributing to the community for fear the bad actor will target them. Quietly, for reasons we never hear about, new members disengage and lapse because of the behavior of bad actors.

Because this can be such a big issue, I reached out to the association community and had some frank discussions with executives who have experience in this area. They say bad actors can create a no-win situation. On one hand, many members dislike the bad actors' behaviors and wish they would go away. On the other hand, leaders fear that if the big association entity shuts down a single member, it may be interpreted negatively.

While there seems to be no one-size-fits-all solution, experts agree that addressing it head-on is best. Some associations create mechanisms for members and staff to elevate issues of bad behavior to the CEO or board president. Conversations between people at the highest levels of the association and the bad actor can produce some positive results. Sometimes the bad actor doesn't realize how their words affect others, and they're willing to make an apology to the whole community. Sometimes, like a tick, they dig in harder. When bad actors indicate they're going to continue their negative behavior, it might be time to review the bylaws and "fire" them from the community.

The bottom line is when leaders do the hard thing by addressing and removing bad actors, other members may notice and may feel proud to be a part of an association that appropriately deals with misconduct. Take this fictional scenario as an example.

The conversation in the online forum was going so smoothly until Alan posted a response to someone's question. Alan's comment seemed to smack down Julie, the thread's initiator, as well as some of the other respondents. It was so caustic; the words were almost painful to read. Julie wondered what was going to happen. She didn't have to wait long because the CEO wrote the next message: "Alan and I just had a very productive chat. He had an unusual experience around this topic and will be taking some time to explain that experience and where he is coming from. We will be hearing from Alan soon." In Alan's message, he apologized and noted that he answered in a way that didn't align with the community's values or his own. Julie was thoroughly captivated because in her organization, bad behavior, like the kind that Alan had originally demonstrated, was simply ignored.

Bad actors can take up a ton of time and mental energy. To the best of your ability, don't let them take you away from the important work of engaging the rest of your members.

Almost 99.997 percent of your members want to help, belong, and connect. Often, they just need a little nudge to participate, and then they'll take it from there. Members report that after they participate a few times, participation becomes a habit. They don't think twice before leaving a comment, asking a question, sharing an answer, or typing furiously in the chat. Over time, trickles of participation turn into streams of participation, and eventually deep participation turns into contribution.

4

contribute

"We ourselves feel that what we are doing is just a drop in the ocean. But if that drop was not in the ocean, I think the ocean would be less because of that missing drop."

MOTHER TERESA

KAT GAZES at the picture of her son on her desk, wondering if she should accept this new, exciting but also uncomfortable opportunity.

This morning, Kat received an email from Anthony, someone in the association's education department. Anthony said he'd been watching the forums and noticed that many of Kat's contributions received lots of interest from other community members. Anthony listed a few of the posts he was particularly interested in, and Kat noted that they were all about the long-running project that Kat had nicknamed "The Beast," which she loved, hated, and loved to hate, depending on the day.

Anthony wondered if Kat had thought about speaking at an upcoming conference: "I think members want to hear about what you are working on." The compliments are nice and it sure is an honor to be asked to speak at this premier event, but the moment Anthony made his request, Kat felt a great gnawing pit of doubt open up in her mind.

Kat has a complicated history with public speaking. When she first came to the company, her boss noticed Kat's quietness in staff meetings and nagged her to speak more. "Don't think about what you are going to say. Just jump in," he would say. "In this environment, people notice whether you speak up or not, and they'll think you're not hungry if you remain quiet!" Kat's style was to think everything through and then state her opinion, so finding a spot to interject during these loud, fast, and sometimes heated meetings remained difficult for some time.

With steel will and sheer determination, Kat started putting herself out there. She jumped into staff conversations whenever she had the opportunity. She led meetings. She volunteered to present her team's work to management. Now Kat doesn't even think about having to make off-the-cuff contributions; they happen naturally.

But public speaking still gives her the jitters. A few years ago, Kat presented at a company-wide meeting. On a stage. With a microphone. Three minutes before she was due on stage, she looked at the route she was supposed to take over big electrical cables and, after speaking, back down some stairs. What if she tripped? What if her knees gave out mid-speech? What if she actually barfed on stage? None of these things happened, but as the emcee was busy introducing Kat, she mentally calculated that the chance of her barfing was about 50 percent.

If she still experienced horrible pre-presentation trepidation talking on her home turf, to friends and colleagues, how much worse would it be at an industry event in front of a bunch of strangers?

Aside from feeling like a scaredy-cat, Kat rationalizes, time is a real consideration. She already works late most nights and misses time with her son. She doesn't need more things on her plate that will pull her away from her family. Presentations, particularly good presentations, take time to create and rehearse. Given her public-speaking fears, she's sure she would need extra time to prepare.

Kat is torn about her response to Anthony. She decides to sleep on it.

During some podcast or another, Kat heard a quote that resonated: "If it is not a *'hell yes,'* it is a *'no.'*" The next morning, Kat mentally runs through the Hell Yes Test and scores a no.

"Anthony, thanks so much for reaching out and considering me for a speaking opportunity. I hear such great things about your conferences and would love to participate, but with my busy work schedule, I won't be able to find the time to create a quality talk. Maybe next year?"

Anthony is used to this kind of response, and he isn't dissuaded. He hopes he can work with Kat to find a format that isn't such a heavy lift and will still provide a great learning experience.

"What about one of our twenty-minute quick sessions?" he asks. Intrigued, Kat thinks about the counteroffer but decides that it isn't enough time to do the topic justice.

"What if, instead of presentation-style, we switch to interview-style? We'll set you up with a great interviewer and you just focus on answering the questions." Ah! Now this opportunity appeals to Kat. She won't have to spend a ton of time preparing, and there's something about the proposed format that doesn't kick her public-speaking fears into high alert. Kat agrees, and Anthony adds another speaker to his list. He's excited about Kat's session and can't wait to see what members will think.

· · · · ·

MEMBERS MAY spend days, months, or years casually participating, and when they're ready, they may want to make a more significant contribution.

Contributors are authors, speakers, interviewees, frequent online community discussion starters, and respondents. Contributing feels more personal than participation because members are putting their work, thoughts, and maybe even feelings on display.

There's an urban myth that most people would rather die than stand up in front of a group of people to speak. I think most people would rather stay on this side of the ground, thank you very much, but public speaking, for many people, is still a tummy-fluttering, knee-shaking, palm-sweating, frightening undertaking. Writing scares the socks off people, too, even those who have been in their career for a long time.

When people think about writing or taking the stage, negative self-talk tends to kick in. Future authors may wonder, *Are my writing skills good enough for a professional piece like this?* Speakers may fear flopping on stage. Sometimes all that self-talk can get carried away!

Will anyone care?

Will they like me?

Am I good enough?

Self-talk can make people brittle. A little bit of constructive criticism can feel like a judgmental blow that stops engagement right in its tracks.

There are high stakes for the association at this stage too. If contribution feels impossible or unappealing, associations may lose valuable content and members. Newer and younger members often feel like there's a glass ceiling preventing them from contributing. With people on the staff, board, or a committee acting as gatekeepers, less experienced members may worry they'll be passed over in favor of someone with more name recognition. At the same time, longtime members sometimes experience burnout due to constant requests to contribute. Either scenario might make members retrace their steps or disengage from the association completely.

How can an association make contribution feel achievable and open to everyone? How can we help people feel proud of and valued for their contributions, and deal with irrational and hidden self-talk? How can we help the community support our contributors as they generously put their ideas into the world?

Cheer On Members

It might seem like "Our call for speakers is open" or "I'd like to interview you for the association's publication" should be enough encouragement for most members. But remember, the invisible goblin on your member's shoulder might be whispering in their ear, *If you don't do this well, you will look silly.*

Instead of dragging contributors along as they slam on the breaks, association leaders can make the experience fun and rewarding by cheering on members.

One organizer I know made it her mission to get new voices to contribute to conference programing. She started attending monthly member roundtable meetings and listened very closely to the conversations. When someone asked a very interesting question or told a compelling story that generated peer response, she'd make a note.

After the event, she'd seek out those folks and learn more about their experiences. If they had a story she thought other members would want to hear, she wouldn't say, "Have you thought about presenting at the annual conference?" Instead, she might say, "Your experience is so interesting, and I have a hunch that many members will find what you have to say unique and thought-provoking. I'd love for you to submit a short proposal to speak at the annual conference. This topic will likely interest the selection committee. Can I send you some more information?"

Cheering on members may give them the confidence to contribute for the first time—or it may be the support someone needs to contribute again and again and again. As an example, here's a follow-up email a journalist sent after a member interview:

> Thank you so much for such a great conversation! I was fascinated by your account of the process you implemented and your focus on your staff's mindset as you all transitioned into something new. The article should publish in just about a week, and I'll send you a link so you will know when it is live. I really enjoyed our chat!

Check out the podcasting world for more great ideas we can adapt. When introducing their guests, hosts often add their own personal remarks to the guests' bios: "This was such a fascinating conversation; I could have talked to them for hours" or "I've wanted to interview this expert for years."

Perhaps editors could preface member-authored articles with some positive language about the contributor or idea? When staff, volunteer leaders, or sponsors introduce speakers, maybe they could add a sentence of appreciation to the bio that the speaker is not expecting? Every time a community moderator, like Kat's Susan, chimes in with a well-placed "What an interesting idea" or "I'm so happy to see you asking this question," they, too, are cheering on members. If these ideas don't fit with your association's style, consider the casual setting of social media, where you may be able to add these personal words of encouragement more readily.

One of the happy side effects of cheering on members publicly is that other members see this too. When they see that contributors are valued, they might warm up to the idea of contributing themselves. Or maybe they'll jump on the cheerleading bandwagon. *Go, go M-E-M-B-E-R-S! We love you!* Soon you may find your members are giving each other heartfelt pats on the back (metaphorical ones, that is).

Teach People How to Contribute

Okay, so, say you've been cheering on members, but finding quality submissions is still a big ol' hassle. There's an answer for that too; not every proposal to contribute is going to meet the criteria, but more of them could.

Sometimes associations fall into a situation where the same members or member companies snap up all the opportunities to submit articles, speak at events, or even win all the awards, while new voices go unheard. Perhaps they are not being heard for a good reason: their proposals don't check all the boxes.

Many associations struggle with this very issue in their journals. A couple of elite member organizations dominate the journal articles while few other submitters get their articles accepted. Sometimes the rejected submitters don't know why their articles are rejected, so they don't know how to improve them.

Here is an interesting secret (or not-so-secret secret) I learned while talking to members whose associations publish journals. It is common practice for elite member organizations to teach their staff how to submit a journal-worthy article. If you happen to work for an elite organization, you may receive the benefit of mentoring, training, or grooming. Those who don't work for the elite organizations likely don't have those handy resources to learn how to produce articles that meet the criteria.

Some associations have remedied this issue by making the criteria for journal articles more transparent and by teaching prospective submitters how to construct a quality article. Even a handful of tips, on topics like how to construct a great headline, and a few links to the various styles of popular articles can help new authors construct a better piece.

Session speakers may need support as well. Most submitters are not professional speakers (and are literally shaking in their shoes at the thought of standing up in front of a crowd). Make sure all the criteria for proposals are public, and consider going a step further with speaker training for those who opt in. A half hour's worth of quick tips can go a long way in helping first-time speakers feel more confident.

At the beginning of the pandemic, most conference speakers were incredibly, impressively, extraordinarily nervous about adapting their talks to the virtual environment. I built a temporary side business conducting speaker training to make presentations more engaging and speakers more comfortable. Whether your speakers are presenting IRL or virtually, live or in a recording, make sure they know how to prepare their content and their environment. Here are some ideas to share:

- **Create engaging slides:** When you make them simple and attractive and vary the format, PowerPoint slides can be engaging. Try to alternate short text (think: words or a short phrase versus a bulleted list) with simple charts, statistics, illustrations, images, or pictures. Also feel free to use props. I often hold up the real book that I'm quoting or referencing a statistic from.

- **Set up your speaking area for success:** If you are presenting virtually, grab lamps from other rooms and place them in front of you on either side. Stack up some big books to elevate your computer's camera to eye level. Wear a headset or earbuds. If you are presenting in person, bring your presentation on a thumb drive in case of any last-minute tech issues. Buy HDMI adaptors if you have a Mac. (I also learned that one the hard way.) And ladies especially, consider wearing an outfit with a sturdy belt and blazer that will give you a place to clip and hide the microphone transmitter, freeing up your hands.

- Embrace interactivity: Grab and hold your audience's attention with meaningful interaction that helps them learn your material. Virtually, encourage participation in the chat. If you are presenting in real time, ask questions and take breaks from your content to read and respond to your audience's thoughts. While speaking in person, ask for a show of hands or get people to shout out short answers, and think about how tech can boost interaction between you and your audience. (Piccles is one of my favorite tools for building engagement fast.)

Experiment with New Formats

Many association leaders worry that people don't seem to want to contribute the way they used to. My theory is while our work lives have changed (more responsibility means less time for associations), the ways in which members can contribute to their professional community have stayed the same. It might be time to add new models of contribution.

One conference that I attended had three keynote spots, but the format of each keynote was very different. The first was interview style: an industry celebrity answered an empathetic moderator's questions, along with curated questions from the audience. The second was a typical keynote presentation. And the third was a roundtable session where trained table leads facilitated the smaller groups' conversations, distilled each group's knowledge into three pithy sentences, and, in rapid succession, presented these insights to the whole audience.

To create more models of contribution, experiment with new formats and consider reducing the time required from members to make a quality contribution.

Because there's a greater need for short-form snackable content, you might find you have more opportunities for micro-contributors. How about asking a member for a ten-minute interview or sending an email with only two interview questions? Ask contributors to record a video of themselves giving one quick thirty-second tip. Or pull answers from the online forum and repurpose them in your articles (asking permission first and giving credit where it's due, of course!).

Do you find that some topics in your online community don't receive a diversity of quality responses? Perhaps expert panels can be established to answer submissions like these.

Contributions can come in all shapes and sizes. Most associations are well acquainted with content contributors, but there are experience contributors too. These are the folks in your association who, perhaps without being asked, act like hosts at your events. They are the connectors introducing members to each other. They might be the first to volunteer to staff the registration desk or to introduce speakers at your conferences.

What other roles can you devise for experience contributors?

Someone asked me recently what I view as the most important technological development for associations. I said, "Zoom chat." Their chin dropped and eyes goggled. I know, I know! Chat?!?! What could be more ubiquitous or boring? But here's the thing: great chats make virtual events ten times more engaging. Adept experience contributors can offer significant value by serving as chat moderators. Chat moderators can:

- Warm up the crowd before an event
- Welcome attendees
- Welcome new members
- Spot interesting conversations and raise them up
- Cheer on participants
- Support speakers by repeating important thoughts
- Keep the conversation going with well-placed answers and questions

A lively chat energizes participants. Designated chat moderators play a huge role in getting more people to participate and share their ideas. And as we talked about in chapter 2, a good chat moderator will supply attendees with positive culture cues and demonstrate additive behaviors.

Some associations ask volunteers to make new-member welcome calls or greet people at the registration desk or reception line. (How might you replicate this dynamic in your online events?)

Experience contributors need training too. Demonstrate how to greet attendees at the registration desk. Provide rough scripts and even video demos to show contributors how to conduct new-member calls. Model how to be a successful chat moderator before the event starts.

Say the More, the Merrier
. . . .

"I have no idea why they turned down my article. It's not so different from the others," bemoaned one PhD. It's heartbreaking to listen to the all-too-common member story of trying to contribute and being told no. I hear a jumble of emotions—often anger, resignation, and sorrow. No matter how rejections are worded, they bruise egos.

After a member's session proposal is turned down, they may never, ever, not in a million years submit again. Even ten years later when they have the skills, credibility, the research, or a really, really good topic to discuss, they may not bother trying.

When only a very limited number of members are allowed to contribute, everybody loses. What if the call for contributors was always open and applying came with a 100 percent success rate? Perhaps you can reengage these folks with rejected proposals by asking them to contribute in a different way. Even if their presentation isn't suitable for a one-hour session, the submitter might make a great article author or podcast guest. Can you offer alternate opportunities for each denied submitter?

Are there other members in your association who aren't often tapped to contribute? Who are they? Young members? Women? People of color? People who don't speak English or are learning the language? They might have an interesting perspective on the ways your profession, industry, or field is changing. What can you do to create contribution opportunities for them? Maybe you could highlight their ideas and work using member spotlights?

Consultants, vendors, and sponsors are another often underused group who are eager to contribute with content and help you warm up the member experience. Many of your sponsor and vendor contacts are in sales. People in this role tend to be naturally outgoing and motivated to build relationships. Make it a win-win by putting them in positions where they can connect with members.

It's possible to create an association culture in which every member can be an experience contributor. Some associations encourage all members to act as hosts. My forty-person-strong Toastmasters club did this, and a publishing association that I know of does too. Before the start of a meeting, during receptions and in hallways, members deliberately look for folks they haven't met yet. They take the initiative to introduce themselves. Once they start talking, introductions to other members are made as appropriate. It's not only the association leaders or staff members who are the event hosts; they have created a group norm of "Hey, you've been to some of our meetings—you should act like a host too!"

Once people have contributed for the first time, we want them to contribute again and again. Rewards can be used to inspire them.

Reward Your Contributors

There is a tendency in associations to give boards a lot of gratitude. Sometimes the conference committee receives accolades too. But most contributors are left out of the public expressions of thanks. This can be a turnoff for those who've spent hours (sometimes hundreds of hours) contributing. Associations desperately need contributors to create volumes of content, and some of that content is extremely time-consuming to produce; a lack of gratitude can have negative consequences for associations as well as for the members whose effort has gone unrecognized.

One colleague who has spoken at over one hundred conferences recounted this story about the positive effect gratitude can have. At the beginning of the conference, her association's CEO took the main stage. She expected the CEO to thank the conference committee, which they did, but then they reminded everyone that the conference could not have been put on without the contribution of their sponsors, exhibitors, *and* speakers. The CEO went on to acknowledge the association's reliance on these members, the value they provide, and the time they take to champion the association and industry. My colleague was so pleasantly surprised by this acknowledgement that she told me the story on a few separate occasions. You go, kindhearted CEO!

A short, sweet, heartfelt public thank-you goes a long way toward ensuring that contributors feel like they've made an impact. Cards, chocolates, photos, and other remembrances of the event can be welcome too.

Helping members get their contribution noticed is also appreciated. Alerting contributors that their recording, article, or white paper has been published allows them to share links to their work with their network. Posts, tweets, and newsletter mentions after an event or publication show contributors that the association is supporting them.

The more time and effort a contributor spends, the more effort you may want to put into commemorating their contribution. And the same goes for the next two stages. The more time, money, or mental energy a member puts into collaborating or leading or volunteering, the more effusive we may want to be with our gratitude. Your best contributors may be ready to become your best collaborators!

As I look into the mysterious, swirling depths of my crystal ball, it predicts that you are going to be one amazing Chief Experience Officer! Now we are going to head into one of my favorite topics. Admittedly, all of these topics are my favorite topics, but this next one happens to be my favoritest topic. (Which is kind of like saying infinity squared, but there you have it.)

5

collaborate

"Finally, there's one other thing that I think every person or frog needs to be creative: friends. For me, the best part of creativity is collaborating with friends and colleagues. Mine happen to be bears, pigs, rats, and penguins, but you go with what works for you."

KERMIT THE FROG

KAT SIGHS in exasperation. Everyone at the conference had just been subjected to another motivational keynote speaker who spent thirty minutes literally shouting at them in an attempt to capture their attention. Now her mind is wandering as she sits in her first breakout session of the day.

The session speaker, from a far bigger organization than Kat's, is talking about the latest, shiniest technological trend. With their resources, it's no wonder they have found success. Until the technology gets a lot cheaper and easier to manage, Kat and her team would have to make do with what they had. When she had picked this session, she'd hoped she would learn at least one new strategy that would apply to her. Not yet. So far, the speaker has just rehashed everything she'd already heard. Such a waste of time.

Why aren't we talking about the big problems? she wonders. *Why aren't we talking about how far behind most of our organizations are regarding HR issues? Or about how our companies are stingy with their work-from-home policies? We all know working from home works. What about diversity and inclusion? We say the words but are only paying lip service. How about parental leave policies that are at least in line with other industries'? I can't keep my youngest recruits because they leave for other industries once they see how old-school ours is. These old mindsets are going to kill our field. Why aren't we talking about these issues too?*

Kat reflects on her run at the association. She's so grateful for all the support and information she got through the association in the early years. Lately, though, it has been falling kind of flat. She's toying with the idea of putting together a peer group for a handful of women who have the same role as her in other organizations, but time constraints are an issue now more than ever. She imagines that together the peer group could solve the world's problems just like she and her friends do over wine at their annual beach vacation. She wishes that someone else would organize the group so she could just join.

• • • • •

STRONG RELATIONSHIPS can form when people work together. I met one of my best friends the first week of my freshman year of college. We fell into step during a five-mile tryout run for the crew team. While significantly out of breath, we still managed a gasping, nonstop, far-ranging conversation more common for a long-standing friendship than a brand new one. After that run, we were inseparable. During our time on the crew team, we ran, worked out, rowed, studied, and ate together. Working hard together and supporting each other during college crew forged a decades-long relationship.

Since then, I've seen a similar thing happen in my professional life. I've completed projects, served on boards, and worked side by side with people who became very good friends. I believe it's because of the work that we became so close. I'm part of a group of four we've dubbed the "Former Ladies of the Board" because we met while serving on the board for our kids' charter school. Even though our terms are long over, we still meet monthly to talk about life, love, work, and happiness.

One of the reasons networking gets a bad rap is that it can be difficult to make lasting relationships out of fleeting interactions. However, members may find they're able to start and maintain meaningful relationships while collaborating.

Not only is collaborating a friend-making endeavor, it's also often exactly what longtime members are looking for professionally. As members advance in their careers, they tend to encounter enormous, hairy, stinky problems to which there are seemingly no solutions. These problems tend to be pervasive. Many members or member organizations have the same significant problem that impacts them often. Some members throw up their hands. Most complain. But others, knowing they haven't found a suitable solution yet, want to band together with their peers to find answers.

Instead of leaving it up to these members to create opportunities to collaborate outside of the association, let's invite them to collaborate within the association.

Amplify More Voices

Sage-on-the-stage presentations are the go-to format for many association events. This teaching model works for some learners and some topics sometimes, but not for all topics or all members all the time.

Take the mid- to high-level professionals. They tell me they tend to feel association programming is very repetitive. Because of their career experience, they might not need training as much as they need to grapple with tough, thorny problems. Longtime members are especially overscheduled, and any seeming waste of time stresses them out. Listening to a speaker drone on and on about a topic that is not relevant is frustrating. These same professionals tend to find association articles and other forms of content less interesting too. Once they reach a certain stage in their member journey and career, they may have a been-there-done-that feeling each time they interact with the association.

A sage-on-the-stage style of presentation doesn't always meet the needs of an association's newest members either. By elevating one speaker—usually an expert with many years of experience in the industry—and requiring the audience to be passive during lectures, we don't make room for young professionals to contribute their valuable knowledge, experiences, and opinions. And many longtime members yearn to learn what young professionals are thinking.

We may not be amplifying enough voices or serving all of our members as well as we could be because our go-to format limits us.

That's been true for a long time. Then came the pandemic, which has sped up some of the trends that, prior to COVID-19, had only been a whisper in our ears. In the early days, nearly all conferences and meetings went virtual, and we suddenly had proof that passive consumption of presentations isn't all that effective—for older members, younger members, and everyone in between.

Attendees tried to multitask, and phone calls, emails, messaging apps, and even social media pulled them away from a traditional webinar-style presentation. While interviewing members, I often heard them say, "I wish the association would stop speaking at me and let me be a part of the discussion." Many associations discovered the same plea in their metrics. Traditional presentations didn't hold attention as well as speakers who created a dialogue with participants in the chat.

Likely there's a large number of your members who would tell you, if they could, "Let's have fewer lectures and more discussion, please."

Help Your Innovators Help Everyone

Over the course of twelve interviews, I had been listening to CEOs' increasingly desperate stories about an industry that was experiencing skyrocketing costs and dramatic drops in revenue at the same time that more government regulations were being introduced. These CEOs had been around long enough that they remembered the good old glory days. Now, they were facing a totally new reality, and I could feel the frustration, anger, sadness, and despair flowing out of the phone along with their words. They were caught between a rock and a hard place, and there didn't seem to be any way to turn things around for these organizations. Or so I thought until I talked to Ana.

Right away the conversation with Ana sounded and felt different. She talked about experiments and projects she had started to deal with some of the big problems the others had mentioned. She seemed to be matter-of-fact, even slightly optimistic about the future, not defeated. It wasn't that Ana had on blinders. She knew the problems intimately;

it was just that she felt there had to be solutions. During our conversation, she mentioned that the association wasn't serving members as well as it used to. "We just keep rehashing the same old challenges!" she exclaimed. "We all know exactly what these challenges are. Now it is time to turn to finding solutions." When I called, Ana was in the process of contacting other like-minded CEOs to see if they wanted to collaborate to tackle these big, seemingly insolvable problems that plagued them. In every research study that I've conducted, I have met people like Ana. I call them innovators.

Every association has members who are tired of talking about a problem and want to get on with solving it. Innovators may have tried to solve the problem by themselves and failed. Or they may have had a small bit of success. Or they know their small resources can't put a dent in the problem, so they are ready to collaborate with peers to find a solution. I estimate that as much as 10 percent of your member population falls firmly into the innovator category. The trick is to mobilize this group.

First, you need to identify the most pressing problem to solve.

What ongoing critical problems have been plaguing your profession, industry, or field? Is it consolidation, regulations, technology, rising costs, pricing, staffing? Sometimes thorny issues have been prickly problems for years or even decades. Sometimes the problem is looming out there in the future like a suffocating, caustic fog no one can see through. What is worrying your members? What tsunami is bearing down on you, poised to crash within the next few years?

Early on, perhaps you heard your industry thought leaders sounding the alarm. "This *thing* is coming our way. You are not moving fast enough. Please listen!" they said. Now that the problem has arrived, you likely hear people pontif-icating about it. Panels discuss the issues and impact, the problem is batted around over drinks, many heads shake, but no real headway is made. Most members moan and groan about the unfairness and yearn for the old days.

Innovators feel the same way (minus the moaning and groaning), but they also want to do something about the problem. They may not have even an inkling of a solution, but they'd like to be a part of it. Innovators tend to be the bellwether for your profession, field, or industry, so it can benefit the association a lot to help innovators convene.

How do you find these innovators? There's probably no metric or data point that will point you to this segment of your membership. But it's not hard to find them.

Just put out the call. Like beautiful moths attracted by the moon, your innovators can't help but be enchanted by the problem you set before them and by the idea of collaborat-ing with others.

Let your members know you are convening all those inter-ested in solving this problem. Using short simple copy, let them know a bit about the format. There are many problem-solving formats to pick from:

- Working groups: People take on various defined roles and work toward the end goal (e.g., committees, special interest groups).

- Lab: The group finds, brainstorms, and experiments with different solutions (e.g., incubators).

- Conversation: The group discusses each element of the problem to share solutions (e.g., roundtables, think tanks).

- Competition: Teams compete to find the solution in each category or the grand solution (e.g., hack-a-thon, X Prize).

In your call, be very transparent about the time commitment. When, where, and how often will you be meeting? Is work outside of meeting time required? If so, how much?

Start setting the stage. For most participants, this will be a new experience. No longer will they be passive recipients or solo contributors. They will now be in the role of an active collaborator. In the way we prime new members for participation, prime collaborators for collaboration. As we talked about in the "Try progressive participation" section in chapter 3, organize the agenda with icebreakers and easy asks first, and slowly build up to more substantive collaborative activities. I bet your collaborators would love to debate whether it's better to be a dragon or have a dragon.

Choose Your North Star

To spark excitement and inspire people to sign up, come up with a good goal.

The right goal will attract interested members to the cause. It will create energy to start the project. A good goal then becomes the North Star to get the group back on track when they nearly inevitably veer off course.

Years ago, I was the staff liaison for a committee that was assigned a poorly articulated goal. In fact, I can't remember the exact goal, probably something like "to grow membership," but I do remember you could drive a truck through it and interpret it about a million different ways. And I remember how after receiving this wishy-washy unreasonably broad goal from the board, we grappled with it at the committee level. The committee chair, let's call him Robert, started the first meeting with a meandering thirty minutes of individual introductions. Then he said, "Okay, so this is the membership committee. What do we want to do?" I held the phone to my ear and listened to a very long and uncomfortable silence. That committee never really got off the ground, but it did teach me a lot about the need to create solid goals.

We want a goal that stirs people to take action—more of a vision rather than a S.M.A.R.T. goal. I'm not knocking S.M.A.R.T. goals, which can be useful in the right situations. But this level of collaboration is not mechanical or statistically driven. It is more like an organic, amorphous blob, happily growing to contain everyone's ideas.

What does a goal for collaboration look like? It could simply be "We will solve X problem." Our goal for the Virtual Networking Incubator was simple: to find out if virtual networking could be meaningful and fun. This goal inspired over 150 registrations in just a couple of days.

Draft your goal. Revisit it a few times. It's okay to have a couple of versions. Then run your goal by a few industry insiders. Are they excited by it? If you sense excitement from a small handful of people, you probably have the right goal. If not, try again.

This is the goal you will use to market your collaborative opportunity. You and your participants will keep coming back to the goal every time you convene. Use the goal to guide the agenda and conversation each time the group gathers. This is your public goal.

As the collaboration host, you should also develop a private goal that answers this question: How do you want participants to feel during and after collaborating? This second goal has to do with experience, and it is the metaphorical card we have up our sleeve that most of us forget about. When we come back to our private experience goal during our planning and before every opportunity to collaborate, we can't help but create a special experience for our participants.

Sometimes communities develop a collective mood regarding their big problem. You might see your community becoming resigned, so maybe you decide that your private goal is to make them feel empowered. Or perhaps the community is feeling beaten down. A private goal could be to help them feel some hope. Or maybe the community is feeling deadly serious, and this is an opportunity to inject some fun. Try to base your private experience goal on whatever you think your community needs right now.

When we launched the Virtual Networking Incubator, the world was firmly in COVID lockdown. Kids were homeschooling. Most of the population was not yet eligible for the vaccine, and select goods and services were still hard to come by. (My family was half a roll away from running out of toilet paper when we were rescued by an extended family member who'd gotten a hot tip about a store delivery and now was flush with TP.) Within the association community, staff were learning how to work from home, converting in-person events to virtual ones at the speed of light, and losing sleep over a completely disrupted revenue model. To many people, the road ahead felt hopeless, long, and dark. With worry so high and happiness so low, we decided that we wanted people to feel joy while participating in the Incubator. Joy seemed like the antidote to the kind of days we were living through: same old, same old tinged with palpable fear.

Adding joy, if we could, was our private experience goal.

Embrace Silly, Half-Formed Ideas

There is a reason why the rules of brainstorming include "Don't judge" and "Use 'yes, and,' not 'no, but.'" The moment we realize our ideas are being evaluated, we self-censor. We hold back our silliest ideas. We wait until an idea is fully formed before explaining it, or we don't share it at all. When our ideas are being judged, our ideas become safer and smaller. Many professional environments are all judgy like that. Almost everyone has experienced a teacher, professor, leader, manager, or peer smacking down their idea in a shaming sort of way. Once this happens, no one wants to feel that sting again, so in new groups, people tend to clam up.

For our collaboration endeavors, we don't want clams, we want whales. Whales journey tens of thousands of miles. They adventure. We need to inspire an environment of adventure, because at any time during a collaboration, anyone could say something that others perceive as silly. But here's the thing about silly ideas—they're gold! It's the silly ideas that can get the conversation flowing again, and they often serve as the jumping-off point for great ideas. To create meaningful collaborations, we need to make it safe to share half a thought.

When I worked at Crayola, one of the ways we came up with new ideas was to facilitate good old-fashioned brainstorms. We'd gather eight or so of our most creative brainstormers in the room and provide a bunch of food, props, and ground rules. (I hadn't thought of the reverse-ground-rule idea yet.)

Even with our group of longtime brainstormers, the gatherings followed an interesting pattern. Early ideas were safe and expected. By the middle of the session, energy waned, and the idea patter became sparser. As we entered the home stretch, people became almost slaphappy (perhaps out of uncomfortable desperation). Someone would throw out a silly idea that under any other circumstance everyone would dismiss, but then a second person would pick up that idea and add half of an idea to it, and then perhaps a third person would ping off those ideas. The next person would say something like, "Hmmm, you know, all this makes me think about this idea . . ." and then they would deliver *the* idea that would stick! A marketable, clever, new idea.

To reach the silly, carefree, loopy idea stage and to create a cohesive collaborative community—to get people to opt in and want to work with each other—we must ban judgment from our collaborative processes.

Here's an example of how an association dealt with the sometimes mean-spirited, closed-minded criticalness that was pervasive in their industry. They found that many students were leaving the field. Talking to students, they learned that when these students presented their papers during other associations' symposiums, many of the senior experts would belittle the students' work, shaming them. Feeling attacked, some students switched the focus of their research to the same old safe topics that have been studied a million times. Others quit.

The association's leadership decided to address this problem head-on and worked with their longtime members to promote a feeling of safety. At their annual symposium, students present their work and receive good, objective, encouraging feedback for truly innovative research. Students know that this association and symposium are truly unique in the field—a safe bastion of ideas and support. For more suggestions about creating a safe space to share, modeling good behavior, and addressing bad actors, check out chapter 3.

Share Solutions with Your Whole Community

The benefits of collaboration don't have to be limited to the participants; the fruits of their labor can help the larger community as well.

Working groups can write white papers, protocols, articles, and brochures for distribution to the membership at large. Roundtable or think-tank conversations can be edited, and the salient points can be made available to the public. The findings from lab-like or hack-a-thon collaborations can be shared with members in the form of a how-to manual or step-by-step directions.

Making solutions available to the larger community is not always intuitive. Pre-pandemic, when most events were in person, collaborations often happened during serendipitous conversations in a hallway or over a meal. Ideas were exchanged, problems were solved, support was given, and the information stayed with the individuals involved. Now with rapid changes in technology, virtual platforms are positioned to change this dynamic.

When members collaborate virtually, we can record or save their conversations. Sure, there are times when we don't want to record a conversation in order to create a safe space in which to collaborate, but saving the chat is generally not objectionable to participants. The chat can be a rich cornucopia of ideas for both association leadership and the rest of the membership. And the chat can be anonymized, stripped of any identifying data that would lead readers back to a particular person.

As the Virtual Networking Incubator wrapped up, we realized we were sitting on hundreds of pages of chat data. We analyzed the data for patterns and wrote a roundup report called *Host Your Own Meaningful Networking Events*. It is a how-to resource to help event planners, emcees, and speakers create a fun and productive networking environment for participants using the best of what we learned during the Incubator.

Imagine offering your first collaborative problem-solving event. Think of how this event could reengage members who have been part of the association for a while. Now think about how your association could become well known as a leader in your industry, profession, or field by publishing the ground-breaking solutions the group came up with.

Turn Strangers into Friends

It turns out that working together toward a common goal brings people together very quickly. Working side by side, we start to like and trust each other, relationships bud, and bonds are created. Making friends or cultivating close collegial relationships is often a rare and accidental outcome of many association connections, but what if we planned collaborative opportunities where members became friends?

My husband and I planned a DIY wedding. Sixty people were invited for a long weekend on an island off the coast of Maine. To keep the cost of the event down, we reviewed our guest list to see if we could leverage our friends' and family members' unique talents and skills. Even though it was a party, everyone had a job.

My husband's charismatic friend agreed to be the emcee. An organized and responsible aunt oversaw the schedule (and another aunt watched the time to keep the first aunt on track). My friends created a playlist, and my sister burned the songs to CDs. My stepmom brought flowers and styled my hair. A bunch of friends came early to set up tables, chairs, and decorations. Another friend led yoga classes every morning.

When guests who didn't have an official role saw other people helping out, they pitched in too. Someone ran to town to buy a case of mosquito repellant. ("We hope you have as many happy years as you had mosquitos at your wedding" was a common refrain in our guest book.) More flowers arrived. A handful of people became unofficial photographers.

Without us planning it, nearly every guest contributed in some way or another, which was great for us and, as it turns out, great for everyone else. Quickly, our guests who were mostly strangers to each other (not to us, we knew them—just wanted to be clear about that) became friends. My friends from high school were hanging out with my husband's work friends. Cousins were laughing with college friends. Work friends were dancing with our parents and grandparents.

Associations can do more to harness the incredible power of collaboration. What if we encouraged members to bring more of their whole selves to each association interaction? What if we helped knit the community together? Intentionally building relationships might be one of the very best benefits associations can aspire to in our very lonely business world. Associations can offer so many ways to cultivate professional contacts and personal friendships. What ideas do you have for making strangers into friends?

6

lead

"If your actions create a legacy that inspires others to dream more, learn more, do more, and become more, then you are an excellent leader."

DOLLY PARTON

O F THE Fabulous Five—that's what Kat and her four best association friends call themselves—the other four have put in some major volunteering hours in one way or another at the chapter or national level. Kat really doesn't want the responsibility or to make the time commitment. No one ever makes Kat feel bad about her lack of volunteering, but to her it's starting to feel like a giant, angry pimple—ugly and right out there for everyone to see.

There's something about sitting on a board that doesn't intrigue Kat at all. Every time she thinks about board service, she recalls some incidents from fifteen years ago, about the time she joined the association. At maybe her second or third chapter meeting, when Kat still hardly knew anyone, the chapter president tried to recruit her for the board. Kat was a bit taken aback. How could she be on the board when she was such a novice newbie? Soon after that, another board member cornered her at a meeting. Then another emailed her. It felt like they were desperate to dump their thankless leadership roles on someone else. The whole thing left a bad taste in Kat's mouth.

Now Kat knows she would probably make a suitable board member. She's accomplished in her career; she's held many leadership positions in her company; she knows a lot about the industry; and she knows many people inside and outside of the association. Intellectually, she knows she should give back, but she loathes the thought of spending a ton of time behaving like a bureaucratic cog. *What do board members do aside from having secret meetings? Does anything ever happen?*

The board is top of mind today because Tamyra, the association's CEO, has reached out to gauge Kat's interest. Kat feels like she's been dodging the duty for a few years now. Despite Kat's hesitancy, her conversation with Tamyra was interesting. Tamyra talked about the new direction for the board and association, and Kat could hear how excited she was that the association was on the road to becoming more innovative and experimental. Tamyra shared three small successes they'd achieved already, and it did sound like a good start to Kat. Still, Tamyra is contractually bound to say all those good things, right?

As the sun is setting a few days later, Tamyra calls Kat again. Kat pounds the Speaker button as she places a half-eaten yogurt off to the side of her desk.

"Hey, Kat! About a year back I remember you starting a conversation at a roundtable about the HR issues in our industry. You talked about how hard it is to attract new talent, especially diverse new talent. It was a hot topic, but solutions have been few and far between." Tamyra goes on to share details about the new working group initiative the association is starting. These groups would tackle big challenges in the industry. They would be part think tank, part lab as participants looked for ways to solve the problem. Findings would be distributed to the entire member community. "Kat, I was wondering if you would like to lead the first working group, both to solve the recruitment problem we have in this industry and to design the process and prove the concept."

Kat's mind starts racing. This is exactly the meaty kind of challenge she likes to take on. She immediately sees the possibilities for the industry and for her career. She knows at least ten other members who care about this issue, too, and who would make great founding team members. Kat is thankful that Tamyra has a few examples of collaborative efforts to examine so they can select the most effective elements and build a process that works for them. But most of all, Kat is excited. More excited about this opportunity than she has been about anything in a long time. Kat is in!

· · · · ·

VERY ENGAGED members tend to move into the deepest engagement stage and become leaders within the association. These roles vary and can include board member, committee chair, organizer, advocate, innovator, or perhaps even mentor.

There are so many reasons members might consider leading:

- They were asked.
- They want to give back.
- They feel it's their turn.
- They'll be able to tout more credentials.
- They think the experience will be a positive learning opportunity.
- They see opportunities for positive change and want to be a part of it.

Nudge Volunteers to Lead

As potential leaders weigh the decision to step up, there are three questions they often ask themselves. When we anticipate their concerns and try to ease them, there's a much better chance they'll say yes.

Do I have the time?

Isabel thought Stephanie possessed all the ingredients to be a great board member. Stephanie's career experience ticked all the right boxes, she was super friendly and appeared collaborative, and Isabel had seen Stephanie make a presentation and agreed with the direction Stephanie proposed. Stephanie had reached out to Isabel with a question unrelated to the board, and they were wrapping up a thirty-minute call when the conversation wound around to Isabel's work on the board.

Admittedly, Isabel was frustrated because the other board members were not doing what they said they would do, which left Isabel with the tasks of finding, booking, and organizing each month's lunch-and-learn. Yet Isabel didn't really mean to utter, "Yeah, my job has taken a hit because this volunteer role has taken up so much time." The words seemed to escape her mouth before she could stop them. Stephanie had been thinking about raising her hand to be considered for a board role, but upon hearing those fateful words, her interest vanished like a puff of smoke.

Members at this stage express a very strong need to give back to the profession, industry, field, and association by extension. But they are astonishingly, hair-raisingly, overwhelmingly short on time. You may hear prospective leaders asking questions about the time commitment, which is so difficult to express accurately because a volunteer's work-load may vary over the duration of their service, as they move in and out of various roles, and with their own ability to give.

Before joining a board myself, I asked about the time commitment on an average week, and my interviewer said, "Oh, about two hours," which was an understatement of, oh, about eighteen hours, in my experience. I felt a little duped and wondered if I should have asked more board members before joining. You can head off these risks by being as up-front as possible when potential board members ask you this question. To avoid accidentally under- or over-estimating, you might even ask board members to keep track of their hours for a few months.

Will there be a social cost?

Jeremy had been a member for years before he noticed what was going on with the board, and that was only because his association friends started talking about it. Apparently, there was rising discontent that the decisions being made at the board level were not transparent—including how candidates for the board were selected.

Soon after he heard the faint murmurs of dissatisfaction, a handful of members who felt a sense of ownership in the association publicly objected. During the all-member meeting to vote in a few new board members, one particularly bold member interrupted the proceedings to voice his opposition to the way the board seemed to be operating. As he sat down, another member rose and said much the same thing. When a third member chimed in, Jeremy wondered if their challenge had been rehearsed. Nevertheless, he could tell that the members of the board hadn't seen this coming and were absolutely shocked. Perhaps they felt personally attacked.

Jeremy had made so many close friends in the association, more than in his own workplace. He didn't want to be in the board members' shoes. *Yikes,* he thought. *How terrible would it be to have people in my professional family hate me because of my service on the board!*

It's not uncommon for leaders to leave an association right after their term is up. Maybe they burn out. Maybe there's nowhere left to go. And maybe the social cost was too great.

People complain to leaders. They pester them for the inside scoop. Conversations that used to be casual become a minefield because leaders might have a whole swath of confidential information they have to guard. If they stay silent, others may hold a grudge; if they give in to the pressure to share details they shouldn't, they may lose trust.

As tough challenges and unpopular issues come up, it's worth talking about how to save individual leaders from negative social costs. The solutions for every association will be unique, but consider the tools you have to improve transparency, unite as a group, and listen to and communicate with members.

Will I be bored?

When Lily thought of joining the board, what came to mind was all-day meetings staring at charts of financial projections in some fluorescent-lighted, stuffy conference room. *Ugh! Going to the dentist to get my teeth cleaned might be more fun.*

I've heard experts argue that the work of leaders, especially on boards, should be strategic, not tactical. Boards should focus on designing a strategy to pull the association into the future. By contrast, the staff's job is to create an operational plan and execute the board's strategy. Some even argue that the board should focus on the future of the profession or industry and less on the business of the association.

But here's the thing. Every association is unique. Volunteer-led chapters and associations, as well as new or small associations, often need board members who can roll up their sleeves, find a meeting venue, and order snacks. Other associations might be going through a period of great change and need their board to collaborate with staff to successfully manage today's administrative snarl all while steering the association into a happier future. And other associations might be so stable that their volunteer leaders can indeed focus on a long-term strategy. When it comes to a board's focus, one size does not fit all.

But one thing every association can do is think about how to make the work of the board (whatever type of work that may be) intrinsically more fun. Running meetings while sitting around a conference table may be common, but that doesn't mean it's the way it *has* to be done. How about taking the board meeting out of the board room to host it in a more innovative space like an incubator, coworking, or museum space? From the pre-work to the meeting agenda to casual networking time, what can you change to make more moments fun and interesting for the board? As you're planning, think about these words: *play, creativity, humor, rest, enjoyment, adventure*—and add in your own words as well.

Play Matchmaker

Not every potential leader will be a good fit for your board or committee. Some members love the details and challenge of building something tangible. Other members yearn to do the hypothetical, big-picture work of strategy. And each member may be capable of a different level of commitment, so the trick is matching each potential leader with the right role.

Just as we talked about expanding the ways to contribute, let's find more ways to lead. Get creative with this. I'll give you some starting thoughts. Do you have leaders who:

- Have an innovative and creative mindset? Perhaps they could lead a trial run to create a new kind of event, product, or service.

- Demonstrate a natural curiosity? Perhaps they could collaborate on solving a giant, complicated industry- or profession-wide challenge.

- Possess strategic skills? Perhaps they might enjoy peering into the future and planning how to get there.

- Are great at change management? Perhaps they might enjoy consulting with other members or member companies.

How else can potential leaders help the association beyond board and committee work? Once you have some roles mapped out, it's time to find the match.

I'm a big fan of conducting small tests. Try reaching out to a few people who have so far been resistant to your board recruitment pleas. Ask them what kind of work they like and are good at doing. If their skills and interests seem to match up with one of the new roles you've created, do a soft pitch and see what happens.

The more you can update the roles of leaders to make their work more interesting, more rewarding, safer, and less time-consuming, the easier you'll make it for potential leaders to say, "*Yes!* I will lead!"

Recruit at the Right Time

Volunteer recruitment is like a delicate dance on top of a lily pad (I imagine—to my knowledge, I've not lived as a frog in a past life). No request to lead will land well if we ask too often or at the wrong time. Both mistakes tend to make the appeal seem desperate. One association CEO that I talked to said she's learned she needs to adopt a position of strength while recruiting volunteers. Appeals like "We really *need* the help" always backfired for her; the approach of "We're looking for a few great people for very limited spots" worked better.

I know firsthand that it's hard not to feel desperate for volunteers sometimes, and those distressed feelings somehow pour right into our communications, which sends potential leaders running for the hills. A few years back, I led the education and recruitment committee for the school board. I found myself talking up board opportunities all the time to adults I was friendly with in the school community. A few people heard my plea a few too many times. I realized this when one parent, who was on my target list of amazingly talented, high-potential volunteers, sighed.

Members tell me that often when they're asked to lead, it's not the right time or the right opportunity. They are too new to the chapter or association. Their professional or personal life is too busy. They don't know enough about the association yet. They don't want to deal with the politics or hardships the association is going through. The role they're offered is not the right fit for them. To make it more confusing, sometimes prospective leaders send mixed signals and don't say no because they are trying to be nice.

Often, longtime board members who are ready to step down will ask anyone and everyone to lead, even hinting at the possibility to new members at their first meeting. New members think, *Yikes! I have no idea what this association is even about yet!* Perhaps, at their second or third meeting, someone again mentions board service, which makes the new member feel pestered.

On the other hand, some associations seem to have a steady stream of "cool kids" getting all the cushy volunteer opportunities. No matter how much anyone else tries, they are turned down. The process for becoming a leader is not well understood, and it doesn't serve associations when leadership selection is unclear. When we ask members to lead, we need to think carefully about when, how, and how frequently we ask them.

You can try a combined public and private approach to asking. Many associations make leadership opportunities transparent by emailing, posting, and messaging members before and during the recruitment period. They share the timeline, the process, the roles that are available, and the selection criteria. An email is followed up by a blurb in the weekly newsletter and meeting announcements.

Privately, the CEO, staff, and board members can also approach potential top candidates. We often know what skills make for the best leaders on our committees and

boards, in our event-planning efforts, and for the new volunteer roles we've just cooked up. When we notice someone
who has an interest and the right mindset, we can nudge
them to learn a bit more about the position. Rather than
leaving recruitment up to fate, more association leaders are
working hard to find and attract top talent.

Extinguish Burnout

You might have noticed that throughout this book, I've been
talking about how busy everyone is these days. I'm going to
do it one more time because the frantic pace of work and
life is changing *everything* for associations. As members
are being asked to do more and more at work and at home,
many are teetering on the verge of burnout in their jobs,
and those feelings of exhaustion, emptiness, and lack of
motivation can fog their association leadership experience.
What's more, their workload as volunteers might be so time-
consuming, so thankless, and so complex that it pushes
them over the edge.

Burnout is an ever-present risk in all associations, but
it's a particularly big problem for smaller associations and
chapters that are far more reliant on volunteer leaders. Here
are some ideas for heading off burnout.

Limit the scope

"I think I'm a complicator!" muttered a partner of mine. We
were getting ready to roll out a big project, the first of its
kind, and there were another thirty add-on ideas the two
of us wanted to try. Every idea supported the original goal

of the project, but we now had a time-sucking behemoth on our hands.

There is a very human inclination to overcomplicate things. In our good-natured, carefree way, we say, "Wouldn't it be cool if we did this thing too?" and then someone else might say, "I *love* that idea, and how about this?" Before you know it, you've plunked another hundred thousand hours on top of an already massive commitment.

Because of the nature of their work, volunteers are often learning their roles for the very first time. Between our over-complicating natures and relative newness, volunteer roles take up a ton of time. As committees, special interest groups, working groups, and event committees kick off, train leaders to manage time effectively and help them rein in and carefully define the scope of their work.

Sometimes a volunteer leader inherits a burdensome role created by an engaged member who had a lot of time on their hands. Use each leader transition as a chance to adjust the scope of the work.

Allow for shorter terms and flexibility

People can almost always make time for a sprint, but marathons are difficult. My husband is a volunteer leader for our local mountain's ski patrol. He is one year into a three-year term, and he has mentioned a few times that he wishes he was one year into a one-year term. It is often useful for the association to have leader continuity, but it is becoming increasingly challenging for leaders to commit to a role for such a long duration. Depending on bylaws, you might be able to play with term durations. As you create new roles for volunteer leaders, set a variety of term lengths—if a project only takes three months, then there's no reason to peg the term at one year.

Long commitments can be alarming but so can being stuck in the wrong role. Burnout also happens when people and roles are mismatched. Could there be a mechanism for leaders to raise their hands early in their volunteer service and say, "This is not what I thought it would be. Can I try something different?" Just as employees move around in bigger organizations, perhaps leaders could shift around in their volunteer roles, so they don't feel trapped and forced to suffer until their time is up.

Recruit uncommon volunteers

I know one quite large professional association that is entirely volunteer run. They create an annual conference, have certification exams, run special interest groups, create standards, and author white papers, guides, and more. Legions of volunteer leaders are needed to do everything from designing new benefits to writing their new-member on-boarding emails. How do they do it? Retirees are a big part of their volunteer leader force. These retirees bring wisdom, strategic chops, engagement, a healthy network, and time to spare.

Who else might have time, energy, and passion? What about students? Professionals temporarily between jobs? Consultants who are just getting their businesses up and running?

Celebrate Your Successes

The nineteen-month project wrapped up. It was a huge, successful, game-changing project. Jess did a mental happy dance for all of fifteen seconds and then started mourning the end of the era. Sure, the project had been tough, but the team who came together for it was amazing. She loved each and every one of them, respected their skills, and was thankful for the ideas and energy they brought to the project. Each one had at least seven more projects vying for their time as this one ended, and Jess did too. Though there wasn't a moment to spare, she couldn't help but think it was necessary to reunite the team to commemorate their work and outcome. No one ever celebrated these things, but perhaps she should.

Projects are completed, events wrap up, and terms come to an end, and often there's nothing to mark the milestone aside from a tiny thank-you. Event committees receive applause at the conference, and sometimes outgoing board members get a sincere toast. What more can we do? How can we help each volunteer leader celebrate a job well done?

Celebrations might include gifts like herbal tea samplers, fruit baskets, and other consumables, or less tangible rewards, like the team spending the final fifteen minutes of the last meeting reminiscing over their achievement and how much they liked working together. If you've got a little budget, spring for an afternoon of sightseeing or a nice dinner for in-person volunteer teams or send DoorDash gift certificates to members of remote teams so you can all still celebrate together. Celebrations are fun ways of expressing gratitude.

conclusion

"I hope that in this year to come, you make mistakes. Because if you are making mistakes, then you are making new things, trying new things, learning, living, pushing yourself, changing yourself, changing your world. You're doing things you've never done before, and more importantly, you're doing something."

NEIL GAIMAN

AS KAT takes the stage to accept the award, her mind flashes back to her early days with the association. *We've both come a long way, baby!* she thinks.

Thirty years ago, she was a driven semi-workaholic eager to prove herself while battling shyness and some insecurities. During the intervening years, Kat moved organizations and climbed the corporate ladder, growing her skills and experience until becoming the CEO. Kat feels more confident in her decisions every year. She's grown a lot, and her association has evolved tremendously too.

The association has always had a great team. She's never met a staff person who wasn't kind, thoughtful, and accommodating. There was a point when she stopped going to the sessions and would hang out with her association friends instead. But she never left, because these were her peeps! Then the association made a few changes that totally reengaged Kat.

The working groups were fabulous, if she did say so herself. Building on that success, the education team created more collaborative opportunities at many of the events.

Tamyra had managed to finally drag Kat onto the board, and you know what? It was actually pretty interesting. The board spent a lot of time talking about the future of the industry. Kat learned so much from listening to her colleagues and from participating in the collaborative trend-forecasting exercises, some of which she brought back to her organization so her leadership team could more effectively see into the future.

I've made so many friends here, she thinks now, looking out at the crowd and seeing many beaming smiles directed back at her. *This is my professional family!*

· · · · ·

YOU'VE DONE it! You've got the mindset, the tools, and the experimental attitude to start your own journey. So—ahem!—by the power vested in me, I officially confer upon you the title of Chief Experience Officer. Go get 'em, CEO!!!

As you bask in the glory of your new title, let's wind down with a few more ideas to successfully launch you into the great adventure of this new role.

Accept (Grudgingly) That You Can't Please Everyone

Member associations invariably abide by a rough facsimile of Newton's third law. There are people who *love* receptions, and in the very same association, there is an equal and opposite contingent who *loathe* receptions. I've learned that one person's festive and fun gala is another person's anxiety factory. And receptions are not the only things members disagree on; they disagree on everything else too.

Many extroverts yearn for in-person events, while many introverts crave online interactions from the comfort of home. Some members can and want to travel, while members with small budgets, family responsibilities, or health considerations try to minimize travel. Sometimes members want to sit back and listen to an expert, and sometimes they want to be a part of the conversation.

Here's where association leaders must walk the tightrope. How do we develop the right value and create the experiences members love when they disagree so much?

Put On Your Analyst Hat

We can answer this question by first figuring out who we are *not* serving well. For most associations, the new-member experience is not as good as it could be, and this is reflected in new-member retention. Typically, members in their first two years have a far higher lapse rate than all others. For members who make it through this gauntlet, the middle years are grand, but then engagement falls off again for longtime members.

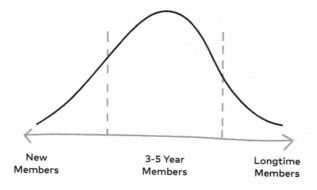

| New Members | 3-5 Year Members | Longtime Members |

This bell curve represents the flow of engagement for most members' journeys in most associations. Be sure to look out for other underserved groups. My research shows that these groups tend to be young parents (particularly women), retirees, students, and members temporarily between jobs. In associations with a global reach, the members who aren't from the association's home country might be less engaged. And don't forget about your segment of innovative members. Are they getting the chance to collaborate to solve the biggest problems, or are they feeling bored sitting in the audience?

What segment of members matters most to the future health of your association, industry, or profession? What can you do to boost their experience?

Okay, so you've picked a segment of your membership whose experience you'd like to improve. What's next?

Well, now you've got to figure out what's going wrong and how to make it right.

A series of questions can help you pinpoint where the experience goes sideways for your segment of members. Try asking yourself:

- What's already working well?

- What's not working well?

- Which touchpoints (e.g., requests to reset the password, registration, etc.) might throw up barriers to engagement?

- Where might our members feel the most unsure?

Now try these questions to reverse-engineer the member experience:

- How can we improve each touchpoint for members?

- Where members feel unsure, how can we address their concerns?

- How can we apply what's working well to what's not working well?

Once you know what's wrong and have a handful of viable ideas for how to fix it, try some small experiments to see if what you're thinking is really going to work.

Try Small Experiments

Whenever associations make a big (or medium or small) pivot, little experiments are a great way to get feedback on your ideas without courting massive catastrophe.

For example, launching a new conference on one specific topic is a colossal experiment. Hosting a one-hour session on the same topic is a little experiment. And you can even go smaller than little if you'd like. Writing an article on that topic—to see if it gains any traction—is a tiny experiment.

Finding the smallest, cheapest, quickest way to test out an idea is a little experiment. In for-profit terms, this is your prototype or your minimum viable product or your tiny bet.

So, how might you use the idea of small experiments to get better at providing great member experiences? Let's say you want to boost collaboration by ultimately producing a collaborative problem-solving event, but a full-scale event with all the bells and whistles will be expensive and time-consuming (read: scarily risky). Perhaps you could conduct your small experiment by convening a one-hour virtual meeting with five interested members. Even at that scale, you can try many of the experience tactics explored in this book, like warming up your welcomes, priming for participation, and making it safe. Lean into your goal of how you want members to feel. Your group is small enough to get great feedback on your efforts.

Speaking of great feedback, are you looking to create more volunteer opportunities? A select group of your members might be willing to act as beta-testers. You could use the same small group of five, ten, or fifteen volunteers for every little experiment, or you could convene a unique group each time. Either way, make sure they know they are experiencing a small experiment and that you are testing something that might or might not work.

Sometimes members feel worried when an association tries something new because they assume there's no going back from it. And sometimes members love the new thing and expect it to be offered permanently. This is another reason for little experiments. Small experiments allow you to see what works without implicitly promising to the whole membership that this is the way things will be from now on.

Every time you conduct a little experiment, you're a first-timer. Even as you scale up, you'll still be new at this, and new means encountering inevitable bumps and flops along the way. But don't worry, I've got your back (and your members have your back too)!

Ask for a Little Goodwill

We want everything to be polished, professional, and perfect for our members. Many associations have a legacy of perfectionism, but flawless execution can often become an insurmountable barrier to change.

Because of the in-person-to-virtual-to-hybrid headless chicken dance we performed in 2020 to 2022 thanks to COVID, members, boards, and staff are now far more willing to ~~endure~~ try new things. And when we let our members know that we're trying something for the first time, that we're taking the risk for them, and that we're experimenting on their behalf, they're willing to accept the inevitable bumps along the way. In turn, they'll give us some grace as we practice.

They might not even notice a blooper or two.

My husband says that I'm a graceful skier, which is funny to me because I often feel like a mess. I suppose he can't see the thought bubble over my head that is often saying, *Yikes!* or *Oops!* or *Gadzooks! How did I get myself on this horrifyingly vertical slope?* Sometimes we look good on the outside even though we feel like a disaster on the inside.

I was on a panel recently where one of the speakers confessed how nervous she felt. Up until that moment, she seemed just as confident as the rest of us. This inside-versus-outside dynamic happens for associations too. A staff team can quickly produce a good but imperfect product, but for members who are experiencing it for the first time, it looks great.

Years ago, in the association community, perfect was the new black. Today, trying new things is the new black. If our members do notice a goof, it's okay, because no one is expecting everything to be perfect. Try new things because bumps and warts are acceptable—often even expected.

Invite a Friend to Be a CEO Too!

At the beginning of the book, I said, "A focus on your members' experiences can start right now. You can do experience work before or in tandem with mission, value, or technology projects. You won't need a big budget (or any budget for that matter). And you don't even need a series of board approvals to make your members' experiences a priority.

"Focusing on your members' experience is not an all-or-nothing game. We're not talking about a huge seismic shift in culture tomorrow. No massive strategic document is needed. Instead, member experience experiments can be as small or as big as you wish, depending on your capacity. As slow or fast too. One person can effectively use these strategies, or you can roll them out to teams or the whole association."

Maybe, as you've read this book, you've started playing with tiny little touches that make your members' experience better. *That is fabulous!!!*

Perhaps you've gotten some positive anecdotal feedback because of your little experiments. Maybe you're ready to take a bigger step toward punching up member experience.

Maybe, ultimately, you'd like to have every member be a co-conspirator in making the member experience great. *This is all music to my ears!*

So, how do you move from the "improving-our-members'-experiences-is-something-that-I'm-doing" phase to the "improving-members'-experiences-is-something-everyone-is-doing" phase? Maybe all you need is just one friend.

Derek Sivers, in his iconic TED Talk "How to Start a Movement," shows that when a leader is joined by one more person, it validates the leader's behavior. (Google this video because it will make your brain happy.)

Find a friend on the staff, on your board, or within the membership, and give them the title of Chief Experience Officer too. Don't worry, there can be one, two, twenty, two hundred, or two thousand CEOs in your association (the Chief Experience Officer kind of CEO, not two thousand of the other kind of CEO—that would just be silly). The more, the merrier. Find your fellow CEOs and together play, experiment, model, welcome, and demonstrate how to create great member experiences. Oh, and have a bunch of fun while you are doing it!

As Lucille Ball said, "Now get the hell out of here and go change the world."

Piglet: "How do you spell 'love'?"
Pooh: "You don't spell it . . . you feel it."

A.A. MILNE

acknowledgments

I AM THE author of this book; however, thousands of other people pointed me in the direction of these big ideas, helped me test strategies, and gave me words for elusive concepts. My gratitude goes out to every person who has answered my questions and shared their feelings and insights with me. A few special people agreed to talk with me about sensitive subjects like bad actors, volunteer burnout, and psychological safety; I won't blow your cover but you know who you are—thank you!

Special partners have enabled me to do really fun and fascinating projects that contributed to my bank of knowledge and the concepts in this book. I can't even adequately express how many thanks go to Maria McDonald and Lisa Vivinetto at Dynamic Benchmarking, Arianna Rehak and the great team at Matchbox Virtual Media, all the wonderful participants who joined us for the Virtual Networking Incubator, and our tech partners. I know you can't see me right now, but I'm doing my jazz hands! Meredith Low, here's looking forward to more Associations of the Future collaborations.

Many wonderful clients trusted me with researching, teaching, learning, experimenting, and collaborating with their members, staff, and colleagues. Special thanks go to Mike Moss, Shelley Wales, Don Boyer, Kim Cannon, Nancy Holland, Anne Ferrante, Coni Fadigan, Andrea Collins, Deb Duffy, Jo Damato, Kate Coscarelli, and those who have switched jobs or retired since our projects together—thank you all! Many, many thanks go to all my association friends whose wise words and curiosity amplified my own.

There are so many brave, innovative, and amazing association professionals whom I learn from all the time, including my dear fellow consultants, and tech, product, and service visionaries—thank you for all your support! This is the best, most collegial, generous, kind, giving community, and I'm proud to call the association industry my intellectual home. Like recipients of Oscars always say, I can't list everyone who has had an influence on me and this work. But I can say thank you to you and you and you!

This book would not be the same without all the care and support from the team at Page Two. A million-bazillion thanks to my editor, Erin Parker, for expending blood, sweat, and tears right along with me. Heaps of appreciation go to Jesse, Chris, Rony, Taysia, Fiona, Crissy, and Amanda.

As a first-time author, I've had tons, piles, buckets full of questions. Mary Byers, Bernadette Jiwa, Jamie Notter, Sherry Budziak, and Mark Collard shared their experiences, and I am grateful to them. Also, as a first-time author, I sure did appreciate all the support, well-wishes, and you-can-do-its from family and friends. Gavin, Mom, Dad, Lida, Molly, Debbie, Jess Taylor, Stephanie Snyder, Stephanie Nieves-Sanchez, Stephanie Prevost (yep, that's three Stephanies—you can imagine how confusing texting gets for me some days), Kimberly Heiman, Kalyna Procyk, Mo Baldwin, and Kim LeClair—thank you to my cheering squad!

In memory of Meredith Anne Huffman, who always knew I was going to do stuff like this far before I did—her steadfast belief will last me a lifetime.

To my husband, Jeff, thank you for always supporting my big dreams.

about the author

AMANDA LEA KAISER is a popular keynote speaker for audiences of association leaders worldwide. As a researcher, author, and Incubator Series cocreator, she is at the forefront of exploring how member engagement is rapidly changing within professional communities. She has been studying and experimenting with engagement for the last twenty-seven years, first as a consumer engagement expert and now as a member engagement specialist. When Amanda is not writing, speaking, experimenting, or researching, she is often exploring a trail, mountain, lake, or ocean with her husband and son. You can find her at AmandaLeaKaiser.com.

elevate engagement

AS A newly minted Chief Engagement Officer, you might be wondering, *How do I get my hands on even more member engagement ideas?* I'm doing a little happy dance because there is so much to explore in the world of member engagement. Here are a few ways to continue your journey.

Get the Latest Resources

Discover a steady stream of new ideas by subscribing to my newsletter at AmandaLeaKaiser.com. You will receive the latest research, like updates to the popular *New Member Engagement Study* and reports like *Host Your Own Meaningful Networking Events*, plus weekly tips on member engagement. Also, by signing up, you will receive invites to events and the latest incubator in the series, which seeks to solve a critical problem in our community.

Share These Insights

Remember I said there can be many, many CEOs (the engagement kind) at your association? Welcome your colleagues to the adventure by sharing this book with them. Buy a few for friends or contact me about bulk orders to gift to volunteer leaders, association professionals, staff, and clients.

Book Me to Speak

My presentations are not your grandmother's webinar. Every virtual or in-person event—whether it's a mind-changing keynote, presentation, innovation lab, problem-solving event, or volunteer leader workshop—combines interactive demonstrations with multiple modes of participation; data, stories, and new ideas; and actionable strategies that participants can start using right away.

Get more information at AmandaLeaKaiser.com.

Printed in the USA
CPSIA information can be obtained
at www.ICGtesting.com
CBHW032249200224
4540CB00003B/13